Privacy and the Information Age

CRITICAL MEDIA STUDIES
Institutions, Politics, and Culture
Series Editor
Andrew Calabrese, University of Colorado

Privacy and the Information Age

Serge Gutwirth
for the Rathenau Institute

Translated by Raf Casert

ROWMAN & LITTLEFIELD PUBLISHERS, INC.
Lanham • Boulder • New York • Oxford

ROWMAN & LITTLEFIELD PUBLISHERS, INC.

Published in the United States of America
by Rowman & Littlefield Publishers, Inc.
4720 Boston Way, Lanham, Maryland 20706
www.rowmanlittlefield.com

12 Hid's Copse Road, Cumnor Hill, Oxford OX2 9JJ, England

British Library Cataloguing in Publication Information Available

Library of Congress Cataloging-in-Publication Data

Gutwirth, Serge.
    [Privacyvrijheid. English]
    Privacy and the information age / by Serge Gutwirth : translated by Raf Casert.
      p. cm.—(Critical media studies)
    Includes bibliographical references and index.
    ISBN 0-7425-1745-4 (alk. paper)—ISBN 0-7425-1746-2 (pbk. : alk. paper)
    1. Privacy, Right of. 2. Data protection—Law and legislation. I. Title.
  II. Series.
    K3263 .G8813   2001
    342′.0858—dc21   2001048625

Printed in the United States of America

♾ ™ The paper used in this publication meets the minimum requirements of American National Standard for Information Sciences—Permanence of Paper for Printed Library Materials, ANSI/NISO Z39.48-1992.

For Maaika and Martin

Contents

∞

Introduction

October 24, 1998, should have been the day. By then, the European Union member states should have brought their national legislation in line with Directive 95/46/EC of the European Parliament and of the Council of 24 October 1995 on the protection of individuals with regard to the processing of personal data and on the free movement of such data.[1] It didn't happen. Halfway through the year 2000, when the original 1998 Dutch version of this book was translated, several European Union member states still had a lot of work ahead of them to meet the conditions.

The directive aims to harmonize the national legislative systems in an attempt to secure the free flow of personal data, which is an internal market requirement. But it should also be seen in light of fundamental rights and freedoms. Additionally, the directive aims to provide a high level of privacy in the European Union.

Doubtless, both aspects truly have an impact. Nevertheless, it is mostly the latter that is stressed, primarily because privacy has positive connotations and appeals to everyone. Not a day goes by without a newspaper writing about an incident directly linked to privacy, and, more often than not, tempers flare when discussions center on the threats facing privacy. So it should come as no surprise that many laws dealing with the processing of personal data have become known as "privacy laws." In name, at least, it gave them a positive thrust.

The European Union directive is not an isolated initiative and contains precious few new ideas. Quite the contrary; it is a perfect extension of the legislative movement that, since the 1970s, has sought to deal with the processing of personal data. From the start, two developments have had a decisive impact on those legislative efforts. One centers on the lightning development of information technology that has created a quantum leap in processing capacity. On the other hand, it has fed the fear that freedom is fast being eroded, as the countless references to George Orwell's 1984 and Aldous Leonard Huxley's *Brave New World* indicate. Reaction was swift and calls were made to safeguard privacy. Indeed, privacy had to be upgraded and reinforced to counter the power of computers and its inherent dangers. In one of Justice's scales are the legitimate processing needs of the public and private sector; in the other rest the private lives of individuals.

The issue of the computerized processing of personal data seems to monopolize the interpretation of privacy. Nowadays, privacy is often defined as the control of individuals over what happens with their personal information. Privacy is purely turned into a check on the gathering, linking, processing, distribution, and communication of data on individuals. It merely sets the limits within which these daunting activities can take place. The question arises whether such a limited perspective is not problematic. Does it allow us to say something about the importance of privacy in our society? Does it allow us to reflect on privacy's role as a core condition for a democratic constitutional state? Does this perspective allow us to tap into privacy's rich history? Doesn't this limited perspective create the risk that certain key questions will not be asked, allowing for the domination of an eroded concept of privacy? Doesn't one run the risk of building on incomplete, skewed, and tendentious preconceived notions? And, does one have to look for a—deliberate or unintentional—hidden agenda?

The ongoing privacy discourse also seems to be largely based on the introduction of technological artifacts, although privacy claims by far precede the introduction of computers. In the past and even now, countless nontechnological situations in which privacy plays a key role have spawned countless words, discussions, and visions. The question remains whether the current privacy discussion addresses the same kind of privacy. Is there no discrepancy between privacy invoked as a buffer against electronic personal data processing and privacy referred to by countless fundamental national and international norms? Doesn't it raise suspicion that the loud and omnipresent privacy discourse—yes, even privacy cult—emerges at a time when the practice and technology of transparency, behavioral control, and influencing is at its zenith of accuracy, de facto reducing privacy to very little indeed? And is this suspicion not further fed by politicians, legal scholars, and business and banking officials using the media to pay lip service to the privacy cult? Or is it because "privacy laws" in fact allow for the wholesale processing of personal data? Does this not again raise the question to what extent the privacy discourse and the new legislation it entails are really aimed at protecting privacy, or whether they are aimed at providing the legal endorsement for the violation of privacy at the service of other interests?

This book does not skirt these questions. On the contrary, it aims to deconstruct and reconstruct the discourse of privacy in light of reflections that go beyond the current controversies on the meaning and/or execution of the current legislation on personal data processing. The book aims to provide the impetus for an enhancing, provocative, and critical assessment on the place, use, and value of privacy in a democratic constitutional state. The point of departure is that privacy is inherently linked to individual freedom, which is essential in such a state. Because of this, privacy affects the core of our concept of law. It also implies that, beyond the deconstruction of a certain privacy discourse, privacy can and must be given a positive and promising content, because it is emancipatory and liberating.

In short, this book does not only aim to be critical and skeptical about obfuscating conceptions of privacy, it also aims to be positive and constructive, stressing the emancipatory power of privacy, which is intimately intertwined with personal freedom. This main objective is covered in the first four chapters. In the book's fifth and final chapter, this approach will be extended to the area of personal data processing and the problems arising from the implementation of the above-mentioned directive. We hope it will provide an impetus to broaden and open up the discussion of data protection in light of an overall reflection on individual freedom and privacy in a democratic constitutional state.

Note

1. *OJ* L281/31 of 23 November 1995.

CHAPTER ONE

Privacy's Complexities

The Many Faces of Privacy

The *Harvard Law Review* published "The Right to Privacy" on December 15, 1890. It turned out to be a seminal article. The piece was a virulent reaction of the renowned legal scholars Samuel Warren and Louis Brandeis against the state of American journalism. They argued that gossip had become a profitable business which showed scant respect for personal feelings and the privacy of sexual relations. Already at this stage, they saw that technological progress and a new entrepreneurial spirit created inadmissible situations which called for effective legal protection. The authors called for privacy, which they defined as "the right to be let alone." It has to be said that the two were outraged by a local rag sheet's brutish treatment of Warren's wife and daughter. Their legal arguments exuded the haughty irritation of the American elite. Yet the article has become a benchmark. It seems that each self-respecting publication on the issue of privacy has to quote it, including this one. It may have less to do with the quality of the legal arguments than with the fact that the article was the first attempt by respected authors to come to grips with the concept of privacy. Brandeis later became an associate justice at the U.S. Supreme Court, an institution which turned "the right to be let alone" into a prime issue.

Gossip, slander, and a prying press relentlessly pursuing and outraging the rich and famous sounds as familiar in the new millennium as it did in the late nineteenth century. The subsequent clamor for more privacy also has a familiar ring. It only goes to prove that the more things change, the more they remain the same. Take the British royal family and the princesses of Monaco. Their bitter tears over lost privacy contrast sharply with the gratification, however dubious, fame brings. Or take the extramarital escapades of leading politicians. The issue goes well beyond Bill Clinton's cigar adventures with Monica Lewinsky, Gary Hart's extramarital fling, or the trials and tribulations of a slew of British ministers. It is just as prevalent in a small state like Belgium. The chairman of the nation's biggest party at the time, the Dutch-speaking Christian Democrat Party, had to quit when it became known that his marriage was on the rocks because of an affair with a famous television reporter. The outrage of the couple over this invasion of privacy had barely died down when, one year later, they appeared all smiles on the cover of a weekly magazine, the willing subjects of a gossipy love story. It proved that the issues of privacy and exhibitionism are full of twists and turns. The attitude of a Belgian vice premier who was accused of being a homosexual and pedophile right in the midst of the Dutroux child sex scandal was much more consistent. It was pretty much an open secret that he was homosexual, and he considered it an intensely private matter which fell under his privacy. The pedophilia allegations increasingly seem to have been a dark political power play. He did not have to resign, but the chairman of the leading opposition party immediately turned it into a very public issue and did not make any attempt to hide his disdain for homosexuals. The leader of the governing Christian Democrats snidely claimed that gays should not be ministers, nor should such a high-profile government official "lead a loose life."

The problem goes well beyond politics. It also applies to society's jet set, including artists, models, athletes, movie and television stars, televangelists, and so on. In Belgium, a gay magazine wanted to "out" the members of the Get Ready pop group, unleashing a stereotypical debate over privacy, press freedom, and homosexual rights, which even became an issue on the restrained public broadcast network. When Pier Paolo Pasolini and Gianni Versace were killed, their homosexuality became an immediate issue, as if passionate murders are a gay penchant. Naomi Campbell's fling with Joaquin Cortes, Celine Dion's worries for her sick partner, Guillermo Vilas's desire for Caroline of Monaco, Michael Jackson's failed marriage to the daughter of Elvis, the stirring passion between Steffi Graf and Andre Agassi—all are public knowledge. Not only because this information can be read in the gossip magazines available in every doctor's waiting room, but simply because it is part of all newspapers and television news programs.

Revealing the privacy of people in the public eye has an unmistakable commercial value. Hordes of paparazzi live off it, and a niche media industry survives on it. It works both ways though and the subjects can sometimes exploit their own privacy for commercial gain: being the willing target of gossip can be lucrative. Private life also has news value. Depending on the public exposure of certain individuals, their privacy can become part of the public domain. If the extramarital affairs of a presidential candidate have an impact on the behavior of the electorate, is this not enough of a reason to make it public knowledge? And what about press freedom, freedom of speech, and the citizen's right to know? The question remains of how far these principles can intrude on the privacy of an individual. Assessing the hierarchal relationship between privacy and freedom of speech and pinpointing the exact divide where one ends and the other starts raise just as many sensitive questions. Each case becomes a high-wire balancing act to define whether the invasion of privacy legitimizes the restrictions on the freedom of speech, and vice versa. The debate has countless arguments for and against, centering on the social value of the information, the people concerned and their privacy claims, the nature of the information, the ultimate goal, et cetera.

Information on sexuality is covered by privacy. Case law considers the following as an invasion of privacy: all revelations on married life; extramarital affairs and partner swapping; the fathering of illegitimate children; visits to prostitutes, peep shows, and striptease bars; the reading and viewing of pornography, et cetera. A logical consequence of this is that sexuality as such is considered a private issue. Sexual behavior is free and should not be steered by rules, regulations, and social norms. Others, specifically the authorities, should not interfere in this. Unfortunately, things are not that self-evident, if only because sex is not that free that it can always stand the light of day. Sexual issues must be dealt with discretely and are constrained to the private sphere. These issues impose privacy, which is evident in the sanctioning of any offense against public decency or morality.

The question also remains, To what extent is sexual freedom covered by the protection of privacy? It obviously is not when the freedom of choice is eliminated, as in case of rape and pedophile sex. The authorities interfere and penalize such behavior. Things are not as clear when it comes to the twilight zone of sexual relations, namely the less obvious or less accepted practices, including oral, anal, lesbian, sadomasochist, or incestuous sex between consenting adults. Is it not excessive meddling to outlaw such voluntary sexual practices? Is the penalization of sodomy not an invasion of privacy? The U.S. Supreme Court decided it was not. In its 1986 ruling in *Bowers vs. Hardwick*, the Court refused to declare unconstitutional a Georgia statute which incriminated anal and oral sodomy between consenting adults. It flatly stated that homosexual sodomy was not a constitutional right and argued that sodomy was not in line with the family and moral traditions of the majority of citizens in Georgia. Justice Harry Blackmun wrote in his virulent, dissenting opinion that the Court missed the point. He argued that the case was about something much more essential, something which needed a positive outcome. It was about the fundamental freedom to manage one's personal intimate relationships, whatever the majority opinion might be. Blackmun pointed out that the U.S. Constitution was exactly about containing the power of the majority. The European Court of Human Rights disagreed with the U.S. Supreme Court, as the cases of *Dudgeon* (1981), *Norris* (1988), and *Modinos* (1993) proved. It ruled that the respective British, Irish, and Cypriot incriminations of sodomy were in violation of the European Convention on Human Rights, which guarantees, in Article 8, the respect for privacy. Sexuality belongs to the most intimate aspects of privacy: a democratic society must have extremely good reasons before it can legitimize such interference. The European Court argued that it did not have any such reason in matters between consenting adults. Sexual freedom comes first, even if a majority condemns such behavior. The United Nations Human Rights Committee took a similar stand when it was faced with a comparable incrimination in Australia's Tasmania. It is noteworthy that in the aforementioned cases the issue is always homosexual sodomy, even if the crime does not require such specification. The reason is simple: heterosexual sodomy is not prosecuted. Justice Blackmun and Michael Hardwick concluded that the Georgia courts did not pursue cases of heterosexual sodomy, even though the penal provision did not differentiate between sexual preferences. It turns out that the protection of privacy is apparently conditioned by the "normality" of the sexual activity at stake.

The European Court of Human Rights took a different stand on sadomasochism. In the case of *Laskey et alii* (1997), it unanimously ruled that, even if sexuality is an integral part of private life, the authorities have a right to intervene when it comes to bodily harm. The authorities are allowed to incriminate such practices, prosecute and establish up to which point the consent of the "victim" covers for the illegality of the act. The interest of public health outweighs privacy.

Transsexuality is yet another controversial matter. Medical and biological progress has allowed people to bring their physical and mental sexuality in sync. This choice for a new identity should be an autonomous decision which falls under the protection of privacy. The consequences of such a change, though, raise a lot of questions. Do the authorities show a lack of respect for privacy when they refuse to change the population register to erase each and every trace of the person's earlier identity? And should the authorities not be forced to do so, since so many current-day activities necessitate identification checks, with gender and first name as essential elements? How is a person supposed to marry, become a parent, travel abroad, and go shopping with identity papers which so obviously disregard the new identity? Even if it is understandable that the authorities cannot interfere in the choice of gender, it is another matter to expect them to actually help in containing the consequences. For a state, abstention—nonaction—is an easier option to deal with than positive action.[1]

The management of the consequences of sex and the choice of individuals on how to live together are at least partly covered by privacy. Marriage, parenthood, family planning, the use of contraceptives, or the decision to have an abortion are all essential decisions in any person's life that should be taken with the largest measure of freedom possible. Again, the same rule applies: government interference should be prohibited unless fundamental interests justify it. Privacy is counterbalanced by the rights of the unborn child, health of an individual, public health, law and order, the core family as a cornerstone of society, et cetera. Other interests are less weighty, such as religious and philosophical objections against birth control, abortion, and premarital intercourse. Clearly nobody is being forced into anything. Everybody can decide for him- or herself, whatever the individual preference. It is exactly this freedom which is an essential part of a constitutional democratic state. It takes precedence over the will of the majority. There are no constraints on birth control in many parts of the world, and it is high time that, in a world blighted by AIDS and extreme poverty, those who still condemn the use of condoms should come to face their moral responsibility. Abortion is legal in most Western states, although legal conditions can vary widely, and is a prime example to illustrate the different ways in which authorities can intervene. The legal status of natural children and those born following artificial insemination, the recognition of nontraditional forms of cohabitation and the adoption of children by unmarried couples are just a few examples the authorities face when they are confronted with the unalienable freedom or autonomy of individuals to choose the way they want to live and raise children. Privacy is the concept which expresses this autonomy of action. Individuals must be able to organize, experience, and enjoy their most intimate and sexual relations without undue interference from other parties.

The authorities must also ensure that this does not entail any undue consequences. Paradoxically, this is why the authorities should be more than mere passive bystanders.

Perhaps even more fundamental is an individual's control over his or her health and survival. The choice of medical assistance is covered by privacy. Without consent, there should be no treatment. This may well be the guiding principle, but public interest allows for some exceptions. Mandatory vaccinations to protect public health illustrate this. The forced sedation of psychiatric patients is possible when those patients pose a risk to themselves or others. Obviously, doctors can also decide that this is the proper medical way to proceed, considering that the patients cannot make a decision for themselves. The preeminence of the consent principle also implies that an individual can prefer a dignified death over an artificial, medical extension of life or a vegetative existence. In the 1990 *Cruzan* case, the U.S. Supreme Court recognized the constitutional right of an able and informed individual to refuse medical assistance and artificial food. When the person concerned can no longer indicate a choice, extremely complex problems arise. Suicide touches on some of the same issues. From a legal viewpoint, suicide is not illegitimate. The individual is in full control of his destiny. Yet this does not exempt from prosecution somebody who fails to intervene or who assists in a suicide.

Privacy also relates to physical integrity and the authority over one's body. Bodily attacks amount to special invasions of privacy. If they are particularly bad, such attacks can be categorized under the provisions of Article 3 of the European Convention on Human Rights (ECHR), which deals with torture or inhuman and degrading treatment. But even the body itself is not fully untouchable. Once a series of conditions are met, the core principle no longer applies. Some obvious examples are the mandatory use of a motorcycle helmet and safety belts, vaccinations, and Breathalyzer and blood tests to check for drunk driving. Criminal law also uses a slew of enforcement methods that disregard the principle of physical integrity. They are justified, though, because they are instrumental in gathering evidence, hunting down suspects, and solving crimes. Obvious examples are fingerprints; body searches; handcuffs; cavity checks; hair and saliva analysis; sperm, blood, and DNA tests; and specific interrogation techniques, including the use of violence. It is obvious that the legal framework and the practical application of such methods are not always fully in accordance with the ECHR. What to think of an investigating judge who orders a DNA test on all males between fifteen and thirty-five of a whole village in an attempt to identify a rapist? What is even more disturbing is the fact that such methods are increasingly applied by private security services, which have long shed any inhibitions to use coercion, including brutal body searches and interrogations. And it is not farfetched to assume that employers and insurance companies rely on the availability of genetic information to screen prospective clients or employees. It raises the specter that a genetic proclivity may cause unemployment or exclusion from insurance services. It can only be hoped that privacy and the bans on discrimination will offer sufficient resistance.

It is only a small step from the inviolability of physical integrity to having control over other aspects of one's personality. A core principle of privacy is the freedom to mold, express, and use one's personality. The picture of a person is still intertwined with the concept of the body itself. Depictions of individuals cannot be produced, disseminated, and commercialized at will, whether it is a drawing, a photo, television pictures, or Web images. The same applies to the voice of an individual. The level of protection will depend on the specifics of each case. A lot will depend on whether the individual concerned gave permission for the use of his or her image or voice, where and how the picture was taken, what kind of picture it is, and what it is used for. There is a world of difference among the picture of a politician on the campaign trail in a quality newspaper, a picture of a nudist beach in a commercial advertising campaign, and a picture of a famous singer such as Jacques Brel withering away on his death bed. Such material again cannot be compared to the reproduction of scenes from a movie, and pictures where the actor does a toothpaste commercial. Mugshots of suspects are different from glossy pictures of soccer stars, as Dutch international striker Patrick Kluivert well knows. (Kluivert was arrested for causing a deadly accident by driving through a red light. Shortly after being released from police custody he again ignored a red light, and at a later time he was arrested on rape charges.) The puppets from Britain's *Spitting Image* or France's *Les Guignols*, two political satire programs that depict politicians, cannot be compared to the use of a picture of a folkloric pageant used to illustrate an article on transvestites. The issue can be pushed to such extremes that a person may object to the display of his or her portrait in the home of the collector who bought the painting. All these issues have one thing in common: privacy is a central theme. Then again, there are no clear, set rules and established legal and intellectual patterns to deal with this. The concept of privacy is something elusive.

The philosophical, social, and cultural choices of a person may be further removed from the physical identity, yet they do shape an individual's personality. Even though the links with freedom of religion and conscience and freedom of expression and education are very clear here, the decisions of an individual that mark or express his or her identity are also affected by privacy. Neither the nation, state, the group, nor anyone else should be allowed to impose or set norms and standards. Privacy gives everybody the freedom to establish an individual path in life and the potential to resist any infringement on this freedom of choice. It is totally irrelevant whether this way of life is predominant or backed by the majority of a nation or group to which the individual belongs. The autonomy of an individual can express itself in dress codes, tattoos, haircuts, piercings, earrings, or three-piece suits. But always, privacy is the common denominator: the right to express oneself. It even goes well beyond this. Everybody has the freedom to create, change, express, or reject a religious, cultural, linguistic, and social identity. The state, however, sets the limits which have to meet constitutional and international standards. Let's take the example of Belgium, a bilingual nation marked by near-constant bickering between the Dutch speakers from Flanders and the Francophones from Wallonia. Following decades of bitter political and nationalistic strife between the linguistic sides, Belgium has been federalized into two language communities which wield considerable authority. Even in so-called bilingual Brussels, every Belgian is forced to choose one or the other linguistic identity. A lot of Belgians though, especially the citizens of Brussels, have enjoyed a bilingual upbringing and now cannot be officially recognized as such. They are forced into a dual, sectarian legal system which totally ignores their bilingualism, a situation which most likely is an invasion of their privacy and probably runs counter to Article 8 of the ECHR.

Minors also face impediments during the search for their identity. Parents can influence, even coerce, them into adopting certain values, partially by selecting a school for them. It is their fundamental freedom and the authorities should keep any interference to an absolute minimum. However, when parents or teachers resort to excessive corporal punishment, the privacy of children will prevail and the authorities will intervene. By the way, parents will soon enough come face-to-face with a youngster's resistance and his or her privacy. In some ways this is almost a comforting, and refreshing, thought.

It cannot be stressed often enough: friendships and personal relationships are an essential part of privacy. Meeting people, deciding who to have drinks with, travel with, with whom to live, who to trust or distrust, who to open oneself up to, and who to befriend are all issues which are so vital yet so underestimated. It is the freedom to engage in a relationship which transcends legal constraints. It has no meaning beyond what the people concerned want to give it. Who doesn't have friends? Who doesn't have unpredictable relationships which can be put into question at any given moment? Who doesn't consider this important? Who hasn't enjoyed the experience of having the mere presence of a friend light up the most boring meeting? The conspiratorial wink of an eye is enough to make the toughest business reunion bearable. Who hasn't enjoyed the unspoken realization that a momentary dispute will not affect a lasting friendship? In short, who should interfere in friendship but friends themselves? Only the most totalitarian regimes dare impose a choice of friendship.

The sanctity of the home is much more a traditional aspect of privacy. That right goes back to the nineteenth-century constitutions, where it is explicitly and independently enshrined. Article 12 of the Dutch constitution guarantees the inviolability of the home. Also, the most important treaties on human rights include in their privacy chapters the protection of the home. A home is inviolable, and any breach of that principle generally engenders criminal prosecution. Once inside a home, people are free from interference by others and the government. It is part of their dignity. A home is a privileged setting where privacy outweighs other considerations. Within a home, each and every one has the utmost freedom to do as he or she pleases, uninhibited by society's social and moral mores. Close the shutters and gone are the prying eyes of others. Loosen that tie, get rid of that skin-tight dress, put some softener on that Mohawk, forget about makeup, relax, strut around in skimpy underwear, pick that nose, show some affection, do nothing, doze off, cry, invite a friend, take a bath together, make love on the kitchen floor. The flip side, though, goes something like this: have a fight, be a tyrant, smash the china, terrorize and abuse the kids, shoot up some heroin. It soon becomes clear that not everything that happens within a home is worthy of protection. Secrets can be ugly, and worse. Still, some behavior which would be deemed unlawful in public is not necessarily so when it happens at home. U.S. case law has already shown, for example, that watching pornography at home and possessing obscene movies which cannot be distributed in public are protected by the inviolability of the home. Providing home entertainment by serving food naked cannot be outlawed in the same way that such entertainment in bars and restaurants is. Alaska's Supreme Court went even further when it ruled that the possession of marijuana at home was protected by the inviolability of the home, even though such possession is considered an offense in other circumstances. This doesn't mean that everything which happens inside the home is automatically protected. Search warrants can be ordered in criminal cases, but only if a series of stringent conditions is met. Hardwick, for example, found no judicial comfort in the privacy of his bedroom when he was caught in the act of "oral sodomy" with a friend. He was held and prosecuted nonetheless. Crimes and unlawful acts are not condoned because they happen to take place within a home. But because a home is granted a special measure of privacy, trespassing by third parties and especially the police and judicial authorities is strictly regulated. The flip side of the coin though is that people without proper housing automatically enjoy less privacy. Clearly, the growing army of homeless, who often spend the night in cardboard boxes, cannot invoke the inviolability of the home when faced with often ruthless and humiliating law-enforcement officers.

It is remarkable to realize that privacy can also apply to environmental issues. When a woman had to be evacuated from her home because of the stench and pollution created by the establishment of a new waste processing plant, she took her case to court. She claimed that her private and family life had been invaded and the privacy of her home violated. She won. The Strasbourg-based European Court of Human Rights also recognized that excessive noise levels from planes and automobiles could, in principle, be considered an invasion of privacy and family life, even if such violations were considered legal. Stench, pollution, noise, and a threat to one's health can affect an individual's privacy.

Much like the inviolability of one's home, the inviolability of the mail is a traditional basic right which is closely aligned with privacy. Nowadays it is often linked to confidentiality of telegrams and telephone conversations, and it is a precursor and part of the more global concept of communication freedom. Interpersonal communication is covered by privacy, and as such, protected from interference by third parties and the authorities. Letters are inviolable and nobody but the intended recipient should be allowed to open them. But here, too, the confidentiality of the mail can be legally violated. This can happen under certain conditions by a qualified person within the framework of a judicial inquiry or in the case of prisoners when there are enough indications of security risks. The latter practice is rife with abuses though. In principle, telephone conversations are secret. They cannot be recorded, registered, or wiretapped. But here too, exceptions are legal if they are part of a criminal investigation. In a series of judgments, the Strasbourg court has established stringent criteria for wiretapping which meet ECHR standards. Combating crime is an obvious legitimate goal, but it does not mean that all police practices to investigate telephone conversations are legal. Disagreement remains on the important issue of whether wiretapping can be used as a proactive precautionary measure, namely to track down illegal action before suspicion has been clearly established. It goes without saying that citizens themselves are not allowed to eavesdrop upon others or wiretap phone conversations. It is a penal offense in many states. But here, too, some exceptions are allowed. In the Netherlands, for example, employers are allowed to listen in on telephone conversations of their staff if they make no "evident abuse" of the practice. Yet it still means that they will face labor law and "civil liability" (tort law) if they disregard the key principles of good employment. In Belgium, no wiretapping or phone recording is allowed unless it is ordered by the examining magistrate. This situation has created a set of rules which is not respected and which has precious little credibility. The letter of the law does not allow employers to check the telephone records in their companies. Hotel owners are not allowed to keep records of outgoing phone calls of their guests. The Belgacom phone company refused to pass on to prosecutors or police services the phone numbers of people who call in with false fire and bomb alarms or make threatening or obscene phone calls. Belgium is hardly the only country facing such tricky issues. Can a phone conversation be taped by one of the callers without the knowledge of the other, for example, as evidence? What about phones which automatically search and register incoming calls (caller ID, call trace, call return, or automatic redial)? Or what about having tape recorders in the room where a phone is picked up? The newest communication technology has only increased the legal problems. It raises the question of whether the rules which govern phone conversations can automatically be extended to include fax, telex, mobile phones, e-mail, data processing, radio and satellite communications, and, obviously, everything which happens on the Internet. If the answer is negative, one can wonder why the protection of privacy of communication would be dependent on technology. In which way is telephone privacy different from e-mail privacy? If the rules can be extended, it is to protect conversation and communication (as such). Doubtless this is primarily so, even if different technologies all create quite distinct situations. But even then, it can hardly be argued that in the end telephone, e-mail, and Internet should all have their independent legal framework. If the issue is communication as such, then bugging a conversation with remote microphones also becomes, mutatis mutandis, an invasion of privacy which might possibly be incriminating. What happens anyway if somebody listens in using a hearing aid? The final step, in theory at least, is that there is no more reason to consider eavesdropping or listening in on a conversation any differently than the telephone conversation itself. It is walking a tightrope between one approach which links the rights and obligations to the use of a specific communication technique to a more fundamental approach which, whatever the medium, is based on the principle of safeguarding the freedom of communication. The latter approach is preferable and should take precedence since it seeks to protect privacy.

It is clear that police and official investigators can legitimately violate the privacy of suspects in an attempt to combat or solve a crime. Sometimes the end must justify the means, but surely not always. Suspects, too, have their right to privacy, all the more since they are presumed innocent until proven guilty. Methods which invade privacy, including wiretapping and house searches, can only be tolerated if they meet a series of formal and substantive conditions which are based on the constitutions and/or international human rights law. According to the ECHR, they have to be foreseen by law, checked by the court during their execution, limited to specific crimes and truly suspect individuals and used only if there are no less intrusive methods available to achieve the same goal. There can be some doubt, however, on the legitimacy once the methods are put into practice. The Dutch Van Traa parliamentary committee, inquiring into the criminal investigation practices of the Dutch police and judicial authorities, was absolutely convinced of this. Numerous investigating methods, such as shadowing, observing, video observation, taking pictures, scanning of mobile phones, and sifting through garbage, are used without any legal basis. Police services often act too much on their own, without any significant control by the judicial system. A posteriori checks by the judge are also found wanting because of the lack of legal norms. On top of that, such intrusive methods are used almost from the start of the investigation, even too early: at such an early stage of a crime that it has more to do with an investigation into someone's intentions rather than with plausible suspicions.

From the outset, the controls on information about individuals have been an important part of the debate on privacy, as has been evident from the many issues which have been dealt with so far. Often it is coined as "informational privacy," and, unjustly, it is sometimes claimed that the whole privacy debate can and should be reduced to exclusively this issue. By the time the reader gets to the end of this book, it should be clear that this is incorrect and undesirable. It is a fact, though, that the collection, storage, processing, or transmission of information about individuals cannot be easily reconciled with privacy. Why? Because the individual is free to decide who knows what about him or her, just as one is free to choose who to be with or how to develop one's personality. Because the processing of information about individuals always opens the door to some sense of control. Because it intimidates. Because people adapt their behavior if it is clear that information is gathered. Because information is inherently linked to power. It is backed up by more than a century of case law of the highest national and international courts. Nobody disputes the fact that privacy is at stake when personal information is used. One important proviso: nobody disputed this fact before the information technology revolution, a development hailed ad nauseam as changing the very core of our society. In fact, Western man did not wait for Von Neuman, Zuse, Jobs, Gates and all the others to realize that police files, medical dossiers, and municipal information are privacy-sensitive. It is already evident in early-nineteenth-century legislation, such as the French 1810 *Code Penal* which imposes professional secrecy on certain professions that deal with personal information. When Nazi Germany obtained the files of Jewish organizations and municipal administrations, probably even the last doubters were convinced that seemingly innocent information—such as name and address—can be privacy-sensitive.

This being said, the importance of information technology should not be underestimated. It ignited the powder keg and brought the issue of "informational privacy" to the fore. When the Dutch government decided in the late 1960s to computerize its population files—with the introduction of a national ID number—and organize a new census, it stirred the nation. And even though the intense protests also expressed the overall social unease of the time, it was specifically targeted against the fearsome specter of power and control that such widespread computerization entailed. The movement gratefully tapped into the many doomsday scenarios of the fledgling technophobic literature, a genre which is, to this day, spawning gloom and doom about the information society. Eventually, the Dutch 1971 census failed because 6 percent of the population decided to boycott it. In neighboring Belgium, the population was faced with a fait accompli. It had the dubious advantage that any protest was hopelessly late. Since 1968, the national register was operating without any legal framework. As a perverse result, legalizing the existing situation turned out to be the only option. In the end, the statute on the national register was "urgently" approved in 1983.

The fear for a quasi-unlimited processing capacity is utterly legitimate. It has nothing to do with diabolical conspiracies. The good intentions of the public and private authorities (improve efficiency and service) don't even have to be put into question. There is the simple fact that it is perfectly possible to collect all computerized information about one individual. It is increasingly easy because of the improvement in quality and capacity of the communication networks and the possible digitalization of all kinds of information (texts, images, sounds, smells, etc.). Consider the following exercise. Suppose—and all this is technically feasible—that the computer system of the civil register is linked to the information systems of banks, the management of electronic fund transfers and banking, and all shops which are part of the system. This alone creates the possibility to know a great deal about an individual, and certainly if that person uses a bankcard regularly. It offers an overview of an individual's activities and movements, but also of income, consumption patterns, and solvency. What can be deduced from the fact that Mr. X uses more gas than he needs for his daily drive to and from work, that he fills up the car during working hours a considerable distance from his work, and that, in the same location, he uses his bankcard at a jeweler, a florist, a restaurant, and a hotel? Think of the fact that supermarkets now use systems that can combine the bank number and product bar codes, allowing staff to know who bought what, where, and when. All this sinks into insignificance when the issue is expanded to include the use of personal information in social security, insurance, health care, advertising, police, and justice. This is to say nothing of the tax collecting agencies, employers, trade unions, political parties, associations, libraries, education, travel agencies, airlines, energy suppliers, phone companies, marketing agencies, headhunters, direct-mail companies, and so on.[2]

To make matters worse, add a slew of cameras and video surveillance systems, which in the end also register personal information, albeit as images: in traffic, city centers, "problem" areas, in the workplace, shops and malls, counters and ticket offices, elevators, hallways, et cetera. The cameras may be hidden, visible or even highlighted. Sometimes they are installed behind mirrors or behind a crack in the wall. Sometimes their presence is pointed out in bold announcements in an attempt at deterrence. Sometimes they transmit images to screens or register them for subsequent use. Individuals too use cameras to register all kinds of images for all kinds of purposes. A motley crew of video fans can be described as any of the following: Peeping Toms; extortionists; detectives; jealous individuals looking to entrap their wayward partner; amateur paparazzi seeking to sell their pictures of disasters, abuse or fights for big bucks; people who do not trust their servants or babysitters; moral crusaders cruising the red-light districts ostensibly filming hookers and their clients; parents who spy on their kids; kids spying on their parents, and so on, ad nauseam. There seemingly is no stopping the surveillance and deterrence functions of mechanical eyes. Jeremy Bentham's unwieldy panoptical building is no match for this.

The conclusion is inescapable. The number of actions of an individual which leave a digital trace is simply dizzying. The massive processing of personal information is threatening to turn us into transparent and easily controlled subjects. The use of uniform identification numbers which make the comparison of information easier only increases this danger. It is a scary prospect and the citizen should rightly demand that information processors give tangible guarantees not to abuse the situation.

So even if the issue of "informational privacy" has not fundamentally changed because of technological developments, the debate has become much more immediate. If manual files were considered to run counter to the privacy principle a century ago, current developments can only reinforce this opinion. We should be lucky that some were not fooled by the philosophical vapor of the "information society" and came to the logical conclusion that our society still is a liberal capitalist constitutional state where privacy is and remains important. Consistent with this viewpoint, they brought privacy face-to-face with its true dangers. And perhaps most of all, they opposed the story, which spread like wildfire, that there is incredible need for haste to ride the wave of the next millennium. The tale goes that law is holding back progress and technology, and needs to recycle itself immediately and fundamentally to meet the challenges of the new and promising "information society." In the same vein, they oppose the widespread assumption that old rules are not adequate to cope with new situations and the law must accept and be subservient to information technology's unbridled possibilities. Move over; there is no stopping technology.

Whether the brave and lucid people of the privacy resistance eventually won their war is dealt with later in this book. One thing is already beyond doubt: during the sixties and seventies, they were able to engender a fundamental debate. Considering the introduction to the many faces of privacy, it was an essential move. By raising the issue of privacy during the debate on the processing of personal information, they aimed far higher than settling for an acceptable compromise. They did nothing less than use the cornerstones of the democratic constitutional state as roadblocks on the ramp leading onto the unrestrained introduction of information technology in the public and private sectors. But did they achieve anything?

The answer to this question requires more reflection on the concept of privacy. The way in which different groups assess privacy as a self-evident positive good is suspicious in a sense, and it requires a more rigorous investigation. The defenders of privacy are spread all over society and it is tough to grasp how they all ended up defending a common cause. The concepts, the stories which win unanimous backing, are often little more than an empty shell. Lip service comes easy. Each and every notion needs to be properly analyzed, whether it is sustainable development, peace, human dignity, or privacy. It is not enough to "deconstruct," to elucidate and confront. The analysis must be able to discover and reinforce the possible critical potential of the concept. This is our objective when it comes to "privacy." Not every evocation of privacy profits individual freedom or the defiance of power. The challenge is to find the wheat hidden in bushels of chaff.

Privacy across Time

Privacy is not a given that mankind has been endowed with since the dawn of time. On the contrary, privacy has developed throughout history. So far, this book has centered exclusively on the contemporary Western notion of privacy. It would be too condescending and too limited in scope to leave it at that, because the concept only has meaning when in interaction with its historical, social, cultural, epistemological, and legal context. Cross-time analysis is called for and hence the reason for elaborating on the development of privacy throughout history.

The historiography of private life has never been easy. The meaning of the term "private" changed from age to age, differed from one social group to another. It makes it difficult to define the subject matter and to pinpoint historical changes and developments. On top of that, any historian is faced with an additional problem: How do we discuss things "private"? How do we find sources? Nevertheless, there is one colorful and virtuoso history of private life available: the five-volume *Histoire de la vie privée* written by a series of renowned historians.[3] It is possible that this history was written because of the important conclusion that language and vocabulary have always expressed a contrast between things public and things private. So historical research into something as intangible as privacy does have a point of departure, even if each society defines, structures, and delineates the notion differently; even if it is subject to changing normative connotations.

During Greco-Roman antiquity, privacy was seen as something negative. The individual who withdraws into the private sphere (one of deprivation) is no better than a slave with no bearing on public life. There is no personal dignity or self-respect without public function or responsibility. To be part of politics is an issue of personal honor for a free man. And he has to invest his personal wealth into this, for example, by organizing plays or building monuments. This self-image is starting to change at the end of the Greco-Roman era. Within a few centuries, it turns into the valorization of Christian self-constraint symbolized by the individual confession. The *homo civicus*, who can only achieve self-fulfillment by controlling the public sphere, is shoved aside by the *homo interior*, who considers self-constraint a goal in itself. One example which marks the change is the development of marriage. A civic duty of the free man to guarantee the succession of a dynasty (pleasure and lust are found elsewhere), it is turned into an individual moral Christian duty shackled by strict rules and totally different values.

The Middle Ages offer a different picture. Feudal fragmentation of power implies a court structure where the lord of the castle stands at the center. He appoints faithful to his court: knights who are in effect integrated into his family. Within society's upper crust, the individual is part of a group within which the public and private characters of his actions merge. The rest of the population, too, is integrated into the feudal structure. Serfdom implies that a lord and his following may determine the fate of their lives at will. Parentage determines servitude, and servitude determines an individual's role. In feudal times, there was little space for privacy because of the paradoxical reason that all power was private. There was no public debate nor public space where the common good was considered or served. Conviviality, communality, and promiscuity made things individually suspect. But as time went by, Christianity carved out a little niche for the individual: the prescribed, regular, individual, and discrete practice of confession forced individuals into solitary introspection.

The foundations of the contemporary perception of privacy are created in the period between the Renaissance and Enlightenment, driven by a series of cultural political events. First, a central state, bent on creating order, reinforces its powers and control over its subjects. Michel Foucault's *grand renfermement*, the wave of imprisonments ahead of the French Revolution, embodies the impact of the state on the individual. Decisions by the administrative police led to the wholesale imprisonment of individuals who disturbed public order, including drunks, rebellious youngsters, whores, madmen, hoodlums, criminals, vagabonds, libertarians, and visionaries of all kinds.

Family too takes center stage as an important link in the pacification and maintenance of public law and order. Family becomes the base where happiness and affection thrive and where social order takes root. On the other hand, though, it becomes the place where discipline is instilled. Yet another important change takes place: the family's private domain, which used to be a poor second to the fame and honor of public life, is upgraded. During the Reformation, the religious movement boosting the individual confession and introspection is also spreading, even beyond the confines of the Roman Catholic Church. Finally, literacy and literature expand the potential of intellectual independence. Even if despots rule, even if the public sphere is lacking, and even if *le secret du roi* still reigns, the conditions for the emergence of the individual sphere are being created.

It is the genesis of "our" privacy, as is evident from the emergence of personal diaries, a general, positive appreciation of loneliness and intimate friendships, and the widespread search for a sense of refinement. Another relevant aspect is Norbert Elias's "civilization process" which conjures up a new relationship between body and mind. Courteousness and etiquette have a civilizing effect on everyday life, much in contrast to the lawlessness of the Middle Ages. Strict constraints gain the upper hand. Sleeping, making love, bathing, defecating, urinating, flatulence, and burping are pushed behind the curtains of social life and are confined to specific places within a home. Social contacts too are subjected to a series of codes calling for formalist, reserved, and terse conduct. In other words, for fear of shame, elementary behavioral norms are interiorized. Self-control and self-constraint rule in an ever more complex society. The interhuman relations are socialized according to the model of the prevailing networks.

In continental Europe, the further development of privacy is only superficially and momentarily interrupted during the French revolutionary years. Suddenly the vast reach of the public powers interferes with private life. Up against the will of the people, the citizen is supposed to be transparent: anything private is suspect and reeks of conspiracy. Nevertheless, the French Revolution and the *Déclaration* lay the foundations for a sharper legal separation between the public and private spheres. Privacy owes to the existence of the fundamental rights and freedoms which can oppose the three constitutional powers. From then on, those powers in turn must be accountable and transparent. It creates, besides individual freedom, a public domain where each and everyone is accountable within the framework of the common cause and the common good.

The aggression on private life during the turbulent years of 1789 to 1794 contributes to the subsequent fallback on the traditional securities and romantic vision of family, home, hearth, and the role patterns that go with this vision. In the early nineteenth century, the family, headed by the unchallenged paterfamilias, becomes the cornerstone of society. It is a small state within the state or a small family within the big family, as described by Jean Étienne Marie Portalis in the *Discours préliminaire* of the *Code Civil.*[4] The family is responsible for the management and preservation of its private economic interests, for the bearing and education of children, the sharing of values and symbols, the normalization of sexuality, for the disciplining of deviant and antagonizing behavior, et cetera. It is the cornerstone and the strength of the state. Wherever family fails, the state intervenes. Poor families are the target of countless measures, including the criminal repression of vagrancy, begging, the gathering of wood, and preventive actions such as charity, benevolence, and patronage. If the family fails in its role to meet the norm, its privacy is quickly up for grabs, too. If it does as expected, the paterfamilias can hold his despotic sway at will. Privacy then quickly comes close to le secret du père (the father's right to privacy.) Nineteenth-century family law completely runs counter to the personal freedom of the family members. Even now, it is hardly privacy friendly. The individual sexual freedom of spouses wanes because of mandatory cohabitation. They lose their personal intimacy and the freedom to make individual decisions on a slew of issues linked to their relation. Children have no privacy whatsoever.

During the nineteenth century, the discontent of youngsters, women, and the artist–intellectual avant-garde increases. The revolt against family goes hand in hand with an upgrading of the individual, personal ambition, and life projects. The core family as the center of power increasingly fails to fulfill its regulating and conformist task. Insecurity, crime, poverty, social unrest, and the ascent of socialism and all proof that the small state within the state has failed to police society. The trend continues during the twentieth century, to the extent that the control on individual behavior, for example, the family, is again being turned over to the state. Child protection, measures against public drunkenness and drug use, wage control, et cetera, are the first legislative steps in this process. They are precursors of the full establishment of the welfare state. Backed by the legitimizing conformity criteria of the social sciences and the aspiration that the making of society can be fully controlled, the state directly addresses the individual through countless government institutions, such as social security, health care, the school system, youth assistance, and so on. Guaranteeing income, eliminating insecurity, offering better perspectives, and providing insurance are all are endeavors that, apart from their immediate good intentions, control and determine individual behavior.[5] But it is not only the family's law and order function which is being affected. The ever-increasing autonomy of individuals also erodes the family from within. Private life turns itself against the family as institution. The all-powerful father loses credibility and is swept off his pedestal. Women, youngsters, and children all gain more freedom. Family ties are no longer predominant and sacrosanct. Other ways of cohabitation emerge. Mobility and the availability of information have never been this abundant, allowing everyone to discover, choose a distinct direction, and be "different." All things considered, a paradox surfaces. The individual thrives exactly at a time when the external controls on his or her behavior are at its peak. The new technological developments in the area of personal information processing and surveillance only increase the paradox. When it comes to privacy, would more be less?

Privacy across Cultures

Cross-cultural analysis is a sobering exercise. The contemporary, Western concept of privacy is not only a relative notion in historical perspective but also when compared to other cultures. Not everywhere in the world are individuals and their freedom, their privacy, and their property considered crucial.

Insofar as sub-Saharan Africa can be assessed as one whole, privacy stands for little. Notably, the 1981 African Charter on Human and Peoples' Rights does not even mention privacy. This contrasts with the 1947 Universal Declaration of Human Rights, to which the African version pledges alliance. Instead, the charter that was ratified by no less than forty-nine African nations highlights African values and traditions, which give content and meaning to human rights. It centers on community, whether this is family, a group, or a people. The individual cannot fully rely on human rights when faced with the group or the state. Rather, human rights are a set of rules which aims to protect the group to which the individual belongs.

Clearly, the status of the individual is limited. The charter gives "peoples" a series of "collective" rights, including the right to exist, to self-determination, and the right to development. Family too is propagated as "the natural unit and basis of society" and the "custodian of morals and traditional values recognized by the community." As a result, the group burdens the individual with duties: duties toward family, community, the state, the international community and other official bodies. This most likely also refers to tribes, clans, parentage, village communities, and other group ties which are traditionally more important in Africa. The extended family dominates and the individual should not disturb its harmonious development. A person has a duty to strengthen the cohesion of the family and owes other family members at all times respect and (financial) support. This mandatory show of respect is so important that it invokes duties which, in Western eyes, are unconventionally included in the charter determining the fundamental rights and freedoms of Africans.

Individualism is subordinate to the group, reducing the space for privacy. In practice, the dominance of the collective spirit probably even exceeds the boundaries set by the charter. This is so, even though many African states shortly after obtaining independence partially or fully adopted the legal system of their colonizers, which was based on the individual. Yet informal law often takes the upper hand, and people prefer the law of the village to that of the state. Most neighborly, family, or interpersonal disputes are solved the traditional way: through discussions and negotiations which involve all members of the local community. As a matter of course, the interests of the group take precedence. The solution to individual conflicts is subordinate to safeguarding the stability of the social context. Chinua Achebe shows in his African trilogy (*Things Fall Apart, No Longer at Ease,* and *Arrow of God*) that solving a murder is much more about finding a settlement between two tribes than a procedure to find and punish the culprit. Such a system makes an individual transparent, to the extent that the physical conditions and the way he or she has to live within the compound have not already done so. An individual's behavior is very much a common cause subject to open and systematic debate. The literature of Achebe and Ben Okri offer us a glimpse into this way of life.

All this has to do with the organization of African society, where the opposition between the individual and the state is secondary. Unlike the situation in the West, everyone is expected to be part of different, strictly hierarchal communities—families, clans, lineage, brotherhoods, et cetera—each of which has specific and complementary tasks. Larger entities, such as the nation-state, aim to pierce this multipolar organization with its plethora of power centers. At most, they can coordinate. Each individual has, according to his or her place and status in each community, specific rights which are linked to his or her duties. To be in a leadership position also means one has to be able to give. People are complementary, not equal. It is hardly imaginable that the Western concept of privacy would fit into such a system. In Africa, it is difficult to conceive a margin of individual freedom of movement alongside, or even going against, those of the powers that be. This would be considered essential in the West. Socially and culturally, this is a barren ground for privacy to take root. Only the state and the legal system can proclaim such a thing. And it can be taken for granted that the rich, Westernized elites will profit from this when it suits them.

The situation is different in Japan. The postwar constitution drafted under the supervision of the Allied forces, especially the United States, had an impact. This is evident when assessing the content and form of the constitutional provisions regarding the fundamental rights of the Japanese citizens. Article 13 of the Japanese constitution, for example, duplicates word for word the Founding Fathers and the U.S. Declaration of Independence of 1776: each Japanese subject is endowed with the unalienable rights to "life, liberty, and the pursuit of happiness." It didn't matter how much this clashed with local tradition. The same article further elevated individualism by explicitly stating that each person should be respected as an individual. The liberal values of the victorious occupier were imprinted on Japanese society through its constitution.

In its extensive list of fundamental rights and freedoms, the Japanese constitution does not specifically mention privacy. Neither does the U.S. Constitution. But in both cases, it does not mean that this right is inexistent. The American judges, primarily the Supreme Court, have confirmed the right to privacy on several occasions and at different levels. The Supreme Court based itself on the spirit—the penumbra—of the Constitution. The Supreme Court refused to give the constitutional list of fundamental rights and freedoms a restrictive interpretation. Japan has gone the same way since the 1960s. The judges of the Japanese high court have recognized the right to privacy even though it is not explicitly mentioned in the Japanese constitution. The equivocal wording of Article 13 allows for an interpretation which guarantees other fundamental rights than those explicitly written down in the constitution. This happened a first time in the case of the great, controversial writer Yukio Mishima, who was to commit ritual suicide following a failed coup. In 1964, Mishima was forced to pay damages because he had referred to the extramarital affairs of a Tokyo politician in his novel *After the Banquet*, in which he mixed fiction and reality. The court based its decision on aforementioned Article 13, which imposes respect for the individual. Japan's highest court also referred to the same article to put the right of portrayal under the privacy denominator.

These halfhearted steps, though, should be taken with a grain of salt. Constitutional individualism and the right to privacy cannot look back upon a long, significant tradition in Japan. Talk of privacy is only three decades old and it is indicative that "privacy" does not have an equivalent in the Japanese language. The English word is used, but with a Japanese pronunciation. One thing is clear, the legal means to enforce privacy claims are much more limited than in the West. Furthermore, in Japan as in most of the Far East, people shy away from settling their disputes in court. To litigate and claim rights has a negative connotation, and generally the parties seek a settlement out of court, based more on their mutual intentions than their mutual rights.

It is beyond doubt that the concept of privacy is on the rise, but questions remain about whether the constitutional ideology is truly entrenched in society. All cause for doubt is justified since individualism as ideology never gained a foothold in Japan. The image is that the individual merges into the "house" or the group. Behavior is determined less by freedom and rights than by loyalty to authority and superiors plus the strict adherence to the behavioral rules. Specific customs need to be respected between employer and employee, between landowner and farmer, between shopkeeper and customer, between citizens and the authorities, between parents and children, between man and wife. These customs are further dependent upon the level of personal attachment between the parties concerned. In other words, the rights of individuals are never indefinitely granted; they are flexible and can adapt to a specific situation. In such a system, loyalty and duty have, understandably, a higher value than rights and freedoms. So even if Japanese constitutional law recognizes privacy, it has no tangible significance for the vast majority, even in the cities. The traditional way still holds sway in modern Japan and privacy finds it extremely hard to take root.

Let us now look at the Muslim world, which is hard to consider as one whole. It is full of religious movements and experiences. A swoop from Iran over Bosnia to Indonesia and Mauritania illustrates the stunning diversity. And that doesn't even touch upon the philosophical differences between third-generation Moroccan immigrants in Amsterdam, Hamas members in Jordan, the Kota Baharu Muslim community and the faithful in a village somewhere in northern Ghana. Human rights issues are assessed very differently throughout the Muslim world, ranging from rabid orthodox rejection to reconciliatory adoption.

It is easy to understand the rejection. In this case, human rights are considered part of the Western secular tradition based upon rationalism, cosmopolitanism, and individualism. Islam, on the other hand, is a religion rooted deeply in tradition and which addresses men and women, Muslims, Christians, Jews, and others differently. The individual is seen more as part of a group and a component of a family or community structure than as an autonomous and independent being. A person must live first by Allah's commands. As a result, duties take precedence over rights and any claim for increased freedom has a touch of subversiveness about it. Seemingly, less rabid positions allow for individual rights and freedoms, yet only if they remain within the limits of religious law, which in Western eyes would render them fairly hollow. It has to be added that orthodox Muslims do not accept that their religious norms are tested by earthly standards. The divine instructions always take precedence, even over the Universal Declaration of Human Rights.

There are movements, on the other hand, that by and large subscribe to human rights law: rationalism, humanism, and individualism are thus part of the Muslim values. These evoke an Islam which no longer badly clashes with the Universal Declaration, and which does not have to take any human rights lessons from a great many secular nations and politicians. From this perspective, many fundamental rights and freedoms seem to find their origin within the sources of Islamic law, and more specifically in the verses of the Koran, Sunna, and the Hadiths of the Prophet. This is certainly so if, as some Muslims argue, the sources have to be progressively interpreted.

All of this creates a kaleidoscope of visions, movements, and national achievements, with sharply varying levels of privacy and individual freedoms. Nevertheless, the 1981 Universal Islamic Declaration of Human Rights, a nonbinding and controversial text, recognizes privacy. The intimate secrets of people need only be known by the Creator and may not be invaded by others. It is doubtful whether this rather limited right to secrecy is comparable with the Western notion of privacy. In Naguib Mahfouz' great Cairo trilogy, the writer shows how despotic relations between a potentate–father and his wife and children can dominate a Muslim household in the Egyptian capital. But this is no different from the countless novels that lay bare the hypocrisy within Western Christian or bourgeois families. Look no further than Thomas Mann's *Buddenbrooks*, Gustave Flaubert's *Madame Bovary*, and Robert Musil's *Der Mann ohne Eigenschaften* (*The Man without Qualities*).

The secularization of the Western constitutional state, however, constitutes a fundamental difference. The impact of religion on the political institutions has strongly decreased, certainly at the official level. As a result, all religions are treated equally, in principle at least. The state does not impose a religious identity. Each and every person has a choice based on the freedom of speech and conscience. Individuals create their own personality free from state interference. Even the majority cannot impose its values. The U.S. Supreme Court has repeatedly confirmed that, whatever people think, it should not be controlled by the government. In *Hardwick*, however, the court made it clear this does not apply to acts, not even the most intimate ones. The European Court of Human Rights in Strasbourg has always stressed the freedom of speech, conscience, religion, and thought. Evidently, there are limits, but they are not imposed by a set of established, substantial values. They are determined by the rights and freedoms of others and by the public interest. Traditional religions such as Islam and Catholicism have a hard time dealing with this, since they basically have clear answers when faced with ethical issues. They speak out clearly, while the state and the so-called value-depleted market fail to make a stand. They claim that common religious values which allow us to differentiate between good and evil truly exist. Fundamental rights and freedoms like privacy are bound by the constraints of what is deemed to be good—in which case the protection of privacy only applies to those who respect religious rules. It comes as no surprise that in times of uncertainty, postmodernism, and economic crisis, such a message is more popular than the tightrope that the secular state constantly has to walk. It is perhaps the reason why there is a strong, and popular, "ethical" movement within the European Social and Christian Democrat Parties. From the viewpoint of the Western concept of privacy, this movement, much as that of the hard-liners within religions, is detrimental.

Contextual Privacy

Let us be very clear on one key point: privacy has multiple meanings. It is not a tangible object that can easily be corralled into a confined definition. Privacy cannot be conjured up by listing a series of human activities. It is not a natural element, nor is it part of reality. It is neither eternal nor universal and it has different consequences in different situations.

Privacy only exists in context, meaning privacy is a relative, contextual concept. It is the complex blend of varying parameters which gives it a certain tenor. Shed privacy of its institutional, social, cultural, religious, historical, and epistemological context, and it becomes a useless, naked notion, bare to the bone.

Privacy is not always, not everywhere, a cherished value. The right to privacy shrivels under the weight of group structure and traditional lifestyle and propriety. It wanes wherever the rights of the individual come in at a poor second to common duty, where gemeinschaft edges out gesellschaft. It need not necessarily refer to Africa or Japan; it can also apply to the Middle Ages, the bourgeois family structure, or the armed forces. Totalitarian governments, despots, and oligarchies also stifle privacy. In short, privacy can only blossom in a spirit of open debate unhindered by political, religious, ethical, or any other kind of dogma.

This does not have to lead to a stark black-and-white vision. There is an immense gray zone in between maximum-privacy and no-privacy societies. Cross-time and cross-cultural perspectives amply illustrate the existence of a slew of variants. *The* Muslim faith, *the* African culture, or *the* Japanese mentality are, in a sense, figments of our imagination since there is always interaction and mixing. Different ideas and opinions, even within a single group, are commonplace. Japan may have totally different behavioral rules, yet the notion of privacy has been established and common problems may well be solved in the same way as in the West. It is important to see whether the values that are safeguarded by the Western notion of privacy are not protected in a different way in other societies. On the other hand, we, in the West, have to question to what extent we indeed did rid ourselves of the traditions, religious beliefs, or values that might impede privacy. We have to scrutinize our own Western system to see whether privacy is truly upheld.

The prevailing concept of privacy, indeed "our" Western version, is embedded in the contemporary democratic constitutional state, the values of individualism, and the constitutional separation between state and church. It is also intimately linked with the idea that individuals are able and willing to unshackle themselves from tradition, social conventions, or religion and dissociate themselves, up to a point, from their roots and upbringing. Privacy is a core concept of a society which wants to guarantee the public interest and social cohesion as well as personal freedom and diversity. The public and private domains have to dovetail without fully overlapping. There has to be a public domain where the common will of the people finds its expression, yet there also has to be room for privacy so that those citizens can enjoy their individual freedom and express their personality. The interaction between the public and private areas is an ongoing process which continuously specifies where both domains link up with each other.

This book may center primarily on the contemporary, Western notion of privacy, but it is not as if narrowing the issue makes things any easier. Even within the Western parameters, privacy has many meanings, remains relative, and is forcibly linked to a context. It applies differently to different people, and the standards for public officials are different from those that apply to Joe Blow, a prisoner, a suspect, a soldier, a minor, or a patient. Privacy changes with location: home, a public road, a private club, a car, or a bar. The impact of privacy is also dependent upon the legal rights and interests it clashes with. Judging violations of privacy depends on motivation: whether privacy was invaded to collect hard news information, seek commercial gain, combat crime, or whether it was merely an act to spread gossip or to stalk someone. Personal relations also have an impact. Relations between strangers, at work, within a family, and among neighbors all create their distinct sense of privacy. In the end, it also depends on the individual. Some people are just oblivious to outside intrusion while others, even though they have nothing to hide, abhor the very possibility of being watched. Some jealously shield their sexual nature and their political and religious convictions while others brandish it. Some consider their body sacred, an untouchable object. Others blot their skin with tattoos, pierce it with rings, sell their sperm, eggs, or kidneys, prostitute themselves, or have silicone implants to look a bit bigger during a wet T-shirt contest. When it comes to privacy, each person has different expectations and different demands.

The notion of privacy remains out of the grasp of every academic chasing it. Even when it is cornered by such additional modifiers as "our" privacy, it still finds a way to remain elusive. This would hardly be expected from a concept linked so closely to the foundations of our society. And let there be no doubt about it: it is a cornerstone of contemporary Western society because it affects individual self-determination; the autonomy of relationships; behavioral independence; existential choices and the development of one's self; spiritual peace of mind; and the ability to resist power and behavioral manipulation. The fact that privacy is beyond words should not be surprising; it is, in fact, an essential characteristic since privacy protects the individual freedom of each and every person. And this, per definition, is beyond definition. Individual freedom can neither be predicted nor conditioned. It is contextual and dependent upon the plethora of meanings it can be given by each and every individual.

Notes

1. For consultation, see the cases *Rees* (1986), *Cossey* (1992), and X, Y, Z (1997), European Court of Human Rights.

2. "Starting with only one or two bits of information (e.g., a name, social security number, date of birth, phone number or address), some firms will search computer databases for current and former addresses, income, education, occupation, employers, age, family status, real estate holdings, business ownerships, foreclosures, bankruptcies, judgments, tax status, liens, cars owned and license plate numbers, driving record, credit history, 'psychographic' information on spending habits and product preferences, pet ownership, names and addresses of neighbors and rental histories mentioned in newspaper articles—and much more." G. T. Marx, "Privacy and Technology," *The World and I* (September 1990): 527.

3. An English translation of *Histoire de la vie privée* (compiled under the supervision of Philipe Aries and Georges Duby) is available. We also relied on works of Norbert Elias and Michel Foucault for further background (see bibliography).

4. Cf. "*Chaque famille est une société particulière et distincte dont le gouvernement importe à la grande famille qui les comprend toutes.*" See also "*Les vertus privées peuvent seules garantir les vertus publiques; et c'est par la petite patrie, qui est la famille, que l'on s'attache à la grande; ce sont les bons pères, les bons maris, les bons fils, qui font les bons citoyens.*"

5. On the welfare state and privacy, see chapter 3.

CHAPTER TWO

The Law on Privacy

The Quest for a Definition

Continental legal scholars have long had a weak spot for definitions. When they write on a legal subject, the scholars usually try from the start to remove any doubt about the words they use and the meanings that the words have. Classical legal works, much like statutes themselves, very often start with a series of definitions, which are used as touchstones throughout the work. It is a fact that there is a good reason to impose such clarity. The application of a legal rule on a practical case will depend on the ability to reduce the case to the terms of the rule: the case has to fit within the definitions of the legal source. When it comes to defining the scope of everyone's rights and duties, clear meaning and definition are essential. It must be clear beyond any doubt who has a right to what from whom.

A similar method has often been used when it comes to privacy. But the contextuality of privacy and its intrinsic elusiveness have complicated the task. A host of legal scholars has failed in its attempts to find a definition of privacy which can be used for legal purposes. On top of that, a profusion of words that can be used to connote the term has only added to the confusion. The availability of such terms as "privacy," "private life," "private sphere," "intimacy," and "secrecy" has certainly increased the number of very subtle, but not necessarily relevant, elaborations on the differences in meaning. In this book, the terms will be used synonymously.

Case law and legal literature on privacy are filled with attempts to define it. But rarely, and never unconditionally, do they yield legally conclusive definitions. The proposals are usually unsatisfactory, even to the authors themselves. In an ironic statement, former French Justice Minister Robert Badinter said that the respect for the secrecy of privacy was apparently such that it was beyond definition. To counter such difficulties, experts often fall back on "a contrario" explanations, which seek to cordon off privacy from the public domain. This method, too, is precarious, and not only because a definition of public domain is just as perplexing. The boundaries between the two spheres move with context and constantly fluctuate. Other legal scholars have given up hope to find a conclusive and coherent description of privacy and rely on classification, categorizing, or listing of the different sub-areas. It has led to the creation of such terms as "physical privacy," "communication privacy," "home-privacy," "informational privacy," and "relational privacy." But even if such concepts allow for the accurate interpretation of some tension areas, the conceptual defragmentation of privacy threatens to lose the core of the term.

This catalog of difficulties is hardly surprising considering what we have seen so far. Privacy, as has been made abundantly clear, is defined by its context and only obtains its true meaning within social relationships. The parameters, which pinpoint privacy and its effects on a situation, are the juxtaposed interests and rights as well as the traits and positions of the people involved. In this sense, privacy is a strategic notion. Its boundaries and limits vary strongly depending on the circumstances and the specifics of each case. Privacy is a concept with a variable content which touches all aspects of life linked to individual freedom. And since that freedom is never absolute, privacy can never offer absolute protection. Not a single aspect of privacy takes absolute precedence over other rights and interests. That includes confidentiality of the mail, physical integrity, and the control over personal information. Never does an individual have absolute control over an aspect of his or her privacy. Individuals do have the freedom to organize life as they please. That will only remain self-evident up to the point that it causes social or intersubjective friction. At that stage, the rights, freedoms, and interests of others, as well as the prerogatives of the authorities, come into play. The friction, tension areas, and conflicts create the need for a careful balancing of the rights and interests which give privacy its meaning and relevance. This intersubjectivity is never totally predictable. And because of this, the definition of privacy for legal purposes is impossible and useless. What's more, it is undesirable. The goal of privacy defies conceptualization because freedom as such cannot be defined. It has to remain indefinable.

In short, the dispute over privacy's definition cannot be settled. This leaves the question of why a slew of intelligent and sophisticated legal scholars has tried, and continues to try, to come up with a precise description and a conclusive definition of the term. One can offer two intertwining explanations. The first is strictly legal and is closely linked to the doctrine which considers privacy a subjective right, namely a "personality right." This is touched upon later in this chapter. From this perspective, a definition is absolutely necessary, because subjective right requires at least a minimal description and understanding of its subject. Hence, the exhausting quarrel over a definition is symptomatic for the inadequacy of this approach. The second explanation has a more philosophical and moral basis. Not everyone is willing to accept that the freedom of others can lead to behavior that he or she condemns. Tolerance and respect for people who are different are not universally accepted norms. Defining privacy's rights will in any case limit the reach and clout of that freedom. This book assesses the issue further, but not until the legal framework of privacy has been outlined.

Privacy in the Sources of Law

Within the Western legal system, privacy is primarily an issue of international and constitutional law. Privacy is mainly protected by explicit provisions, both in international human rights treaties and in the distinct constitutions. In the case of the Netherlands and Belgium, several privacy provisions from international human rights treaties apply. One is Article 12 of the 1948 Universal Declaration of Human Rights.[1] Like the whole declaration, the article is not legally binding for national legal systems, even though it remains a topic of hot debate. Article 17 of the 1966 International Covenant on Civil and Political Rights (ICCPR) is also seeking to protect privacy.[2] And finally, one has to refer to Article 8 of the European Convention on Human Rights (ECHR), which highlights the respect for private life in the European human rights order.[3] Both the ICCPR and the ECHR are binding treaties. On top of that, Article 17 of the ICCPR and Article 8 of the ECHR are self-executing and directly affect the national legal systems. They are incorporated in Dutch and Belgian contemporary law. Both articles take precedence over conflicting internal legislation, including the constitution. They can both be invoked and have to be applied by national judges. In practice, the ICCPR is overshadowed, certainly when it comes to privacy, by the ECHR. The latter is older, has a strong supranational judicial control mechanism, and, last but not least, the Strasbourg Court can boast an impressive list of judgments on privacy. All this makes it legitimate to center attention as of now on the ECHR.

Articles 10 through 13 of the Dutch constitution also refer to privacy. Article 10 contains the general principle of the right to protection of privacy,[4] while the three other articles respectively guarantee the inviolability of the person,[5] the protection of one's home,[6] and the privacy of the mail, telephone, and telegraph.[7] Privacy is a constitutional basic right. It was not formulated as a directive for the authorities, but as a direct and effective right for the citizens.

We can draw several conclusions from these articles. First, whether we are talking about a national constitution or an international human rights treaty, we always face moral rules which are at the top of the norm hierarchy. Privacy therefore touches upon the essential principles of a national legal system. It is at the center of the European human rights order created by the ECHR as well as at the center of the strongest human rights treaty with a global reach. Privacy expresses a fundamental value of our society and the image of man on which this is based.

Second, all aforementioned legal norms use the same phrasing and are equally vague and undefined when it comes to privacy. National and international constitutional legislators alike allow for a wide conceptual area within which privacy can be construed by subordinate legislation or by a judge. The many faces of privacy already gave us an indication of what can be sheltered under privacy's umbrella: communication, the inviolability of the home, the establishment of relationships, physical and mental integrity, the processing of personal information, surveillance, abortion, contraception, family life, family reunification, memberships and affiliation, behavior, and so forth.

Third, the ECHR and the ICCPR primarily deal with "vertical relations," meaning the legal relations between the authorities and the citizens. The basic rights, including privacy, are primarily meant to oppose government action, which must stay within the legal limits set by the ECHR and ICCPR. Privacy is a sword to be used against public authorities.

Fourth, the protection of privacy is never absolute. There are always explicit provisions which make the imposition of restrictions possible. Nevertheless, any meddling in privacy will only be legitimate when a set of conditions are met. These conditions are best defined in Article 8, second paragraph, of the ECHR: the restriction of privacy must be foreseen by law—or an equivalent legal source (the formal criterion); second, the restriction can only be applied when it is considered necessary in a democratic society (the necessity criterion); third, it can only be used to achieve one of the specific and limited goals set out in Article 8 of the ECHR, including public security and the safeguarding of rights and freedoms of others (the legitimacy criterion); fourth, the Strasbourg Court has added the condition that any action must be useful, indispensable and proportional to achieve the set goal (the proportionality criterion). The last standard implies that the established goal could not be reached through measures that would have had a lesser impact on the guaranteed freedom of the individual concerned (subsidiarity criterion). If those conditions are met, the authorities can take measures which constitute an invasion of privacy. If not, the Strasbourg Court can rule that they contravene the ECHR. This, for example, will be the case if a wiretap is ordered without a proper legal framework as required by the formal criteria.

Fifth, privacy requires first and foremost a government hands-off policy, but there is more to it than that. Public authorities also have to take positive action. They have to take legal measures to guarantee privacy. The Dutch constitution is quite explicit when it comes to such positive action. An example is the issue of personal data processing. Article 17 of the ICCPR is just as explicit but its formulation casts the net wider, arguing that, in general, everyone has the right to the protection of the law against interference with one's privacy. The Strasbourg Court too brought Article 8 of the ECHR in line with this approach. Public authorities have to take legal measures to guarantee a meaningful enjoyment of one's privacy. These positive obligations of the state also extend to intra-citizen relations: if the privacy of one individual is threatened by another, the state has to intervene. For example, when it comes to the inviolability of the home, the government has to set rules not only to counter infringements by the public authorities, but also by fellow citizens. Public authorities thus have a paradoxical role to play. On the one hand, they are seen as privacy's main threat, while on the other hand, they have to make sure privacy is respected.

Sixth, Article 8 of the ECHR, Article 17 of the ICCPR, and Article 10 of the Dutch constitution have (to a varying extent) a horizontal effect, meaning that they also have an impact on the relations between individuals. Some scholars, though, have yet to be won over by this legal fact and continue to fight a rear guard action against it. The impact on interpersonal relations is evident when assessing case law. The Dutch Supreme Court, the highest court of the Netherlands, has repeatedly taken decisions that applied privacy in horizontal terms. The person who unjustly invades the privacy of another commits a wrongful act. The legislator has turned this vision into reality by laying down rules for horizontal legal relations against the background of safeguarding privacy, as has been done in the 1988 Dutch Data Registration Act. Despite all legal arguments to the contrary, the horizontal effect of basic rights is self-evident. If privacy is protected against acts of the public authorities, should it "a fortiori" not be protected against individual acts, too? After all, the government acts on behalf of the public interest, which seems to be a more legitimate reason for an invasion of privacy than, for example, personal profit seeking of a businessman. On top of that, the authorities are bound by their legal powers, giving citizens an additional touchstone (misuse of power is, of course, illegal). It raises the question of what the reasons can be to allow individuals more leeway than the public authorities in dealing with the privacy of others. There is no valid reason to give, say, a headhunter more freedom than the government. If privacy is truly a fundamental legal norm, then it must be evident in all legal relations. If not, it erodes the basic right. This is all the more so since personal relations are now just as much based on power as relations with the public authorities. Relations between employers and employees; among banks, insurance companies, big business, and consumers; between landlords and tenants; between health care institutions and patients, et cetera, are often very lopsided. They can be extremely "vertical," increasing the dangers that privacy can be invaded. If the basic rights and freedoms, especially privacy, are truly aimed at protecting the subject's resistance against power, than they must be effective in all power relations that affect the individual. After all, it is the personal freedom of the citizen which is at stake, and this freedom is violated just as much, if not to say more, by a shopkeeper's surveillance cameras as it is by police cameras.

It is obvious that the criteria promoted by Article 8 of the ECHR, assessing the legitimacy of government interference in privacy, need more than a mere transposition to horizontal relations. But the set criteria contain a series of indications which can help a judge assess a dispute between individuals, as case law has already shown. The subsidiarity, proportionality, and necessity criteria imply an examination of whether the infraction is not out of proportion with the established goal. The weight of the rights and/or interests that oppose one another can be assessed based on the provisions of the second paragraph of Article 8 of the ECHR. On the one hand, when it comes to the hierarchy of norms, personal freedom comes out on top. What's on the other hand? The reason why a person invades the privacy of someone else and the seriousness of the infraction are considered. They also are important aspects of the judicial decision-making process. Whatever the circumstances, the judge will have to take all concrete circumstances of the case into account to appraise whether an invasion of privacy was justified.

Privacy: Neither a Personality Right nor a Subjective Right

The opponents of the horizontal effect of privacy included from the start many continental lawyers and legal scholars specialized in private law centering on horizontal legal relations. They see privacy as a "personality right,"[8] a subjective private right with special characteristics. The existence of such a right in positive law, however, is not very clear. It seems more likely that the concept of the personality right owes more to an international theoretical movement, mainly in Germany and France, and a legislative development in France, where since 1970, Article 9 of the *Code Civil* explicitly guarantees everyone's right to a private life. The Netherlands and Belgium, for example, do not have such an article.

According to this theory, personality rights are subjective rights which grant individuals far-reaching control over the components of their personality and personhood. These rights would be an inherent part of an individual, and because of that, they would be phrased as absolute, extra-patrimonial, effective *erga omnes* rights (rights that apply to all) which imply a specific judicial claim. The intended goal is the hope that a violation of the subjective right will automatically be seen as an unlawful act, overturning the onus of proof and avoiding a balancing of interests. The theory is well meaning: the personality rights must reinforce the holder, especially when faced with the interference of other individuals.

A first problem immediately surfaces. A subjective right must have a clear subject, it must serve something which can be sufficiently defined. For example, a patent gives its holder a clear, exclusive right to commercially exploit an invention for a set period of time. The "right to privacy" however, cannot be defined, or only in the vaguest of terms. In a sense, this discussion should stop right here, because a judgment on whether the right to privacy has been violated must in the end fall back upon an analysis of a complex set of facets which come into play (who, what, where, when, why, how, with what purpose, etc.). It means a careful balancing of interests to meet the social criteria of the general duty of care. In short, it means back to square one.

But more is happening here. The plea for a description of privacy as an absolute, inalienable, and extra-patrimonial personality right is open to more profound criticism. For starters, the absolute character of such a right can be put into question. Even if the right to property—the most absolute right—can be limited, the same also goes, mutatis mutandis, for the right to privacy. This is not only because it is vague, but especially because privacy is preeminently contextual and relational. It only acquires a legal significance in a balancing of rights and interests in case-specific circumstances. What's more, the extra-patrimonial character of the right to privacy is far-fetched and obfuscating. Reality has shown that, however ethically deplorable, everything private can be turned into business: the commercialization of nudity, sexuality, intimacy, organs, sperm, egg cells, life stories, victimhood, and so on—anything goes. Each part of privacy can be the subject of agreements and transactions, obviously within the limits of contract law which excludes that an agreement can have an illicit purpose. It can even be said that personality rights create a scarcity of, and thus a true market for, privacy-related goods and information. If a personality right—no matter how much it is defined as extra-patrimonial—is violated, damages will follow. The transgressor will consider whether he or she pays the price. Paradoxically, a possible protection through the use of personality rights will increase the value of personal information.

Nevertheless, it is especially the ideological content of the plea which creates problems. Is it not suspicious that voices for the extra-patrimonial and absolute subjective right to privacy are raised just when the market use of personality components is reaching ever higher levels. What's the point? The answer is clear: control and moralizing. By translating the different aspects of privacy in subjective (personality) rights, individual freedom is forcibly encroached upon. The definition of this right implies that it defines precisely whatever is worthy of protection. The subjective right to privacy must be described beforehand and with a positive formulation. It implies that a hands-off approach no longer suffices. The subject must and shall have a defined and described right to a part of his personality, whatever the context of the conflict. This approach thus implicitly differentiates between protected and nonprotected choices. It is very much the question of whose moral criteria will apply. The judge's? Those of the majority? The one is as dangerous as the other. And to make matters worse, the personality right is conceived as inalienable, creating the situation in which an individual is protected from his own immorality. The law becomes paternalistic.

The theory of personality right creates normative and normalizing interferences in an individual's freedom of self-determination. Freedom however, meets its limitations only in intersubjective relations, not at the level of individual choices. When it comes to intersubjective relations, the law can balance the issues, mediate, modulate or negotiate. When it comes to individual choices, it should simply back off. The attempts to create an unequivocal subjective right to privacy are implicitly based on the wrong assumption that the law has to and is allowed to impose "good values." Sodomy between consenting adults is again a good example to highlight the debate. From the personality right's point of view it can be argued that sodomy, whether homosexual or heterosexual, is not among the values which are deemed worthy of protection by the personality right. Like the U.S. Supreme Court ruled in the *Hardwick* case, sodomy can be punishable as such since there is no subjective personality or basic right covering sodomy. The opposing point of view defends the freedom of privacy, in this particular case, sexual freedom. It is the position that the Strasbourg court took, for example, in *Dudgeon* and *Norris*. Privacy, in these cases, means the absence of legal norms and the individual's responsibility for choices made. Legal considerations are only called for in case of friction or tension. When it comes to sexual freedom as such, it is off-limits for the law.

But the Fundamental Freedom . . .

When it comes to privacy, as we have suggested, law needs a perspective of freedom. Privacy, as François Rigaux has shown with aplomb, is an outstanding expression of an individual's freedom.[9] The "right to privacy" then becomes the "freedom of privacy" or "privacy's freedom." Violations of privacy are not attacks on an "autistic" subjective right, but on the freedom of individuals to experience themselves and their relations with others as they please, void of any interference. Law and society only need to act if the actions resulting from this freedom clash with other interests. The different interests have to be considered against the background of the public interest and the rule of law. It may sound like a paradox, but privacy is relational, intersubjective, and social.

It can be argued that it makes precious little difference in legal practice how privacy is conceptualized. Whether judges base their reasoning on the personality right or on the freedom angle, the elusiveness of privacy will always confront them with the problem of balancing the different interests. Even if this is true in practice, there are nevertheless essential differences. The "subjective right to privacy" is, from the start, an inadequate concept since one cannot have a right to something which cannot be defined nor rendered objective. The credibility of law, fragile as it is, does not need such porous concepts.

On the other hand, privacy as freedom does not create any conceptual headaches. Freedom itself creates the indefinability. What's more is that the personality right discourse creates problems because it is contradictory. The established goal—the free development of the individual—clashes with the means. The elaboration of a subjective right to privacy requires a conceptual and normative freeze of an individual's self-defining process. The freedom approach, however, leaves in the middle what individuals are or should be and how they should behave. Privacy exists because we are different, not because we are all the same. Legal problems occur only when freedoms clash with one another or when the exercise of freedom clashes with the public interest (or vice versa). Last but not least, "the freedom of privacy" seamlessly dovetails with the concept of the pluralist, democratic constitutional state. But this premise needs a more elaborate motivation.

In a Democratic Constitutional State

Alain Touraine explicitly stressed in *Qu'est-ce la démocratie?* that democracy is inextricably linked to pluralism and diversity. It must give as much freedom as possible to as many people as possible and protect the largest possible diversity. There is no democracy without a multitude of viewpoints, opinions, projects, and behavioral patterns. Thus, democracy is distinguished less by the fact that an elected majority rules than by the fact that it limits the powers of this majority. The elected authorities are bound by the fundamental rights and freedoms of each citizen, including those of the minority. Any legislation which runs counter to this principle is either unconstitutional or in violation of international human rights treaties. Equality means that each and every person has the freedom to determine his or her life and personality, even if it goes against what the majority considers "normal" or "morally acceptable." People are equal because they are different.

In such a society, the individual has the leading part. Individuals determine their own identity and have the right, even the political duty, to resist the powers which aim to steer their self-development in a certain direction. Everyone has to be able to autonomously participate in the public domain based on personal self-determination. This implies a strict respect for the freedoms of speech, conscience, and association, and the personal freedom of privacy. "Values," and "absolute truths" have to make way for projects, dialogue, confrontation of ideas, openness, and pluralism.

But at the same time, democracy has to safeguard its survival. Excessive individualism can lead to a disintegration of the whole. Therefore, democracy has to establish a political institutional system within which, paradoxically, cooperation and diversity are possible. Touraine argued that the main challenge of the democratic constitutional state is its ability to make strongly diverse individuals and groups live together in unity. Again, we are faced with a paradox. The constitutional state has to guarantee both maximum freedom and the continuation of the common project, within which this freedom can thrive. In such a venture, tension is essential, because individual freedoms can clash with each other or with the joint project as such. Obviously, such a system cannot function without an autonomous body which permanently mediates between all parties with the aim to establish relatively stable balances.

According to the relational theory of law which René Foqué and A. C. 't Hart established and applied in several legal sectors, this autonomous body is the law and it must mediate between the different social powers and actors. The law continuously reestablishes their relations based on the freedom of the individuals and the control over the common project, which has this freedom as a central theme. The trait of the democratic constitutional state is exactly that power relations can be dealt with based on law, not violence.

The discourse so far implies that individual freedom has to be protected by positive law against infractions committed by the state, other citizens, or legal persons. But this legal point of view also has important consequences when it comes to the relation between the legal concepts and everyday life. If law wants to mediate, it has to avoid both sheer idealism and being a mere stark reflection of reality. Legal concepts are not equivocal and require a conceptual area within which mediation is possible. They have to remain open and allow space for other points of view, other interpretations, other truths. Law should not be monopolized by one dominant social project, world vision, or reflection of reality as if no others are possible or legitimate. In other words, law should not become purely an instrument of government at the service of one cultural, ethical, ethnic, religious, political, scientific, mystic, or whatever sort of ideal. Instead it has to enable the coexistence of different individuals and projects. Such a concept of law turns legal notions into sanctuaries where differences can be freely expressed and debated. The existence of "the other side" must always be considered even in the face of the strongest possible claims, including scientific ones. The law guarantees the expression of resistance, which is the oxygen of democracy. Because of this, law should not impose identity, normality, or "truth." Instead, it should manage differences.

All this does not make law totally relative. The legal system has to survive as a unity, and thus it has to safeguard its own existence. It has to make sure that, on the one hand, it maintains its capacity to mediate, and on the other hand, safeguards the values of the democratic constitutional state. These values—which are per definition relational—meet the double bond of the democratic constitutional state, including respect for fundamental rights and freedoms such as diversity, emancipation, participation, tolerance, reciprocity, and proportionality. So even if the democratic constitutional state needs to be based on the principle of neutrality, this is because of its pluralist and democratic quality, not because of any form of relativism. Pluralism itself, and the tolerance and dialogue that go with it, are values that force the constitutional state into a position of neutrality. But then again, this doesn't mean that the democratic constitutional state should not act against individuals and groups which threaten these values. Sometimes, the democratic state has to show its teeth; for example, in the case of privacy to combat crime or in the case of freedom of speech to counter holocaust negationism.

Therefore, individual freedom is at the heart of the democratic constitutional state. It is not relevant who the individuals are, what they think, or how they assess their personality. Instead, it is important what individuals do, how and when they let their voices be heard, and how they offer resistance within the balance of power. Law only deals with tensions, conflicts, friction, and relations. Individual self-determination and autonomy are always part of social interaction, if only because individuals, their environment, and the events in their lives are permanently intertwined. An identity is always the result of a blend and is never stagnant. This ceaseless, unpredictable, colorful, and dynamic diversity of individuals and groups is the lifeline of the democratic constitutional state. Law has to protect the many successive *métissages* that individuals constantly go through from all forms of absolute claims. Diversity and pluralism are democracy's trump cards.

Privacy is the legal name given to the protection of individual freedom. Hence, privacy is part of the hard core of democracy's project since it guarantees individuals their freedom of self-determination, their right to be different, and their autonomy to engage in relationships. Privacy protects alternative behavior and the resistance to power at a time when it clashes with other interests or with the public interest. Much more than any subjective right, a nonmystifying privacy develops itself as the fundamental freedom of the individual.

Privacy in the Scales of Justice

One thing is absolutely clear by now. In a society like ours, privacy is quintessential, a cornerstone of law. Privacy's freedom is not only a theoretical fundamental value, it is also upheld by the highest legal standards—constitutions and international human rights treaties. Privacy is also crucial in relation with other fundamental rights and freedoms. Indeed, personal freedom is often a condition for the effective enjoyment of those other fundamental rights and freedoms. Unless an individual enjoys freedom of conscience and self-determination, it makes little sense to speak about effective freedom of speech and association. It also works the other way though. Privacy has a sizable impact because it is part of a package of intertwined fundamental rights and freedoms that guarantee our individual, political, and social emancipation.

However, this doesn't have to mean that privacy always has to take precedence over other interests and rights—to the contrary. It is only in exceptional cases, when specific legislation addresses a specific aspect of privacy, that the case as such is beyond doubt and no balancing test is required. The violation of the penal code covering the confidentiality of the mail for example is punishable, whatever the justification. But in a large majority of cases, legislation is not this clear-cut and privacy ends up in the scales of justice. The principle of the hierarchy of norms is not absolute.

There are several good reasons to limit the effect of the hierarchy of norms. First, all freedoms, no matter how fundamental they may be, are limited by the freedoms, rights, and interests of others and the public interest. This was already clearly specified in the *Déclaration des droits de l'homme*, and it is still part of the ECHR (including the second paragraphs of Articles 8, 9, 10, and 11) and has been confirmed in jurisdiction (including the decisions of such constitutional courts as the U.S. Supreme Court and the Strasbourg Court). In a democratic constitutional state, all fundamental freedoms and rights are measured by the strength of the public and private interests with which they clash. Second, the hierarchy is not absolute, because of the elusiveness of the concept of privacy as described above. The limits of freedom can only be determined in intersubjective conflicts because personal freedom is unspecified and privacy is not a specific protected object. As such, privacy is irrelevant: it always has to be seen in context and in relation with the interests and arguments it faces.

Privacy can be limited by "normal" common rights and interests, expanding the scope well beyond the fundamental rights and freedoms and the public interest. There is no decisive difference when it comes to conflicts between norm-hierarchal equal interests and clashes between differing interests. This may not push the whole principle of hierarchies of norms to the sidelines, but it does dent its absolute character. Legal mediation will be necessary in three possible situations—clashes between privacy and other fundamental basic rights (e.g., the freedom of expression or the right to property), clashes between privacy and the public interest (e.g., public security or public health), and clashes between privacy and common rights and interests (e.g., economic interests, the right to process personal information, or the right to have one's life project respected by others).

An imbalance in the hierarchy of norms only comes to the fore in the third case. Economic interests or a moral project and privacy are issues at different levels of the hierarchy of norms. Yet there is a need to mediate. In a balancing test, the legislator or judge must certainly take the predominance of privacy into account. It can probably be said that the balance should shift in the direction of fundamental freedoms. So, if it remains a realistic possibility that the balance eventually tips in favor of, for example, the economic interest of a businessman, one has to make sure that this is subjected to stringent conditions because of the predominance of privacy. In any case, the violation of privacy must be kept to a minimum and the proportionality and necessity criteria will have to be applied. Is it absolutely necessary and essential that privacy is violated to achieve the established goal? Does it cause the least damage to privacy? How and to what extent does the violation of privacy undermine the freedom of citizens? How does it affect behavior? Is the interest at stake important enough to require such measures? What are the privacy expectations of those involved? Is it reasonable to ban the activity for the sake of privacy? What aspects of the specific case should be taken into account?

Interests will always have to be weighed against one another when privacy clashes with other freedoms in the legislative and legal process. The hierarchy of norms will play an important but not absolute role. Because of this, privacy will never take absolute precedence, but it will become more important as the hierarchal level of the "counter-interest" is lower. The implication of this is highlighted in chapter 5, when practical examples and implications from the personal data protection area are assessed.

But first, we need to apply a healthy dose of skepticism.

Notes

1. Art. 12 of the Universal Declaration of Human Rights: "No one shall be subjected to arbitrary interference with his privacy, family, home, or correspondence, nor to attacks upon his honor and reputation. Everyone has the right to the protection of the law against such interference or attacks."

2. Art. 17 of the International Covenant on Civil and Political Rights: "1. No one shall be subjected to arbitrary or unlawful interference with his privacy, family, home, or correspondence, nor to unlawful attacks on his honor and reputation. 2. Everyone has the right to the protection of the law against such interference or attacks."

3. Art. 8 of the ECHR: "(1) Everyone has the right to respect for his private and family life, his home, and his correspondence. (2) There shall be no interference by a public authority with the exercise of this right except such as is in accordance with the law and is necessary in a democratic society in the interests of national security, public safety, or the economic well-being of the country, for the prevention of disorder or crime, for the protection of health or morals, or for the protection of the rights and freedoms of others."

4. Art. 10 of the Dutch constitution: "(1) Everyone shall have the right to respect for his privacy, without prejudice to restrictions laid down by or pursuant to Act of Parliament. (2) Rules to protect privacy shall be laid down by Act of Parliament in connection with the recording and dissemination of personal data. (3) Rules concerning the rights of persons to be informed of data recorded concerning them and of the use that is made thereof, and to have such data corrected shall be laid down by Act of Parliament."

5. Art. 11 of the Dutch constitution: "Everyone shall have the right to inviolability of his person, without prejudice to restrictions laid down by or pursuant to Act of Parliament."

6. Art. 12 of the Dutch constitution: "(1) Entry into a home against the will of the occupant shall be permitted only in the cases laid down by or pursuant to Act of Parliament, by those designated for the purpose by or pursuant to Act of Parliament. (2) Prior identification and notice of purpose shall be required in order to enter a home under the preceding paragraph, subject to the exceptions prescribed by Act of Parliament. A written report of the entry shall be issued to the occupant."

7. Art. 13 of the Dutch constitution: "(1) The privacy of correspondence shall not be violated except, in the cases laid down by Act of Parliament, by order of the courts. (2) The privacy of the telephone and telegraph shall not be violated except, in the cases laid down by Act of Parliament, by or with the authorization of those designated for the purpose by Act of Parliament."

8. There is no equivalent English legal term for "*droit de la personnalité*" (French), "*Persönlichkeitsrecht*" (German), or "*Persoonlijkheidsrecht*" (Dutch). This is due to the fact that the notion is nonexistent in Anglo-Saxon legal systems. We opted for a literal translation of the term as "personality right" (and, for example, not for "rights of personhood") to make clear that the discussion focuses on an actual legal debate in civil law systems. Nevertheless, both the fundamental terms and the issue at stake—how to conceive privacy: in terms of "rights" or in terms of "freedom"?—are also relevant for a fundamental reflection on privacy in Anglo-Saxon legal systems (cf. L. H. Tribe, *American Constitutional Law* [New York: Foundation Press, 1988, chapter 15, 1302–1435]). A thorough *comparative* account of the above-mentioned discussion, including references to the common law systems, is found in F. Rigaux, *La protection de la vie privée et des autres biens de la personnalité* (Brussels: Bruylant/L.G.D.J, 1990, 849 p).

9. *"En bref, la privacy est la liberté individuelle par excellence, elle se situe aux confins de toutes les libertés publiques et de tous les droits civils, mais elle est aussi un signe d'inégalité, l'un des enjeux du droit contemporain étant de convertir un privilège aristocratique en maîtrise de soi-même accessible à tous. Il y va d'un droit à la différence, individuelle et collective."* F. Rigaux, *La protection de la vie privée et des autres biens de la personnalité* (Brussels: Bruylant/L.G.D.J, 1990, 9).

CHAPTER THREE

Ambiguous Privacy

Privacy as an Empty Shell, a Mirage

Such terms as "freedom," "autonomy," "self-determination," and "privacy" have a lofty resonance. And they indeed offer a pretty picture—a free individual who sets out his or her own course in life in a society where all free individuals coexist in a balanced and harmonious system. Maximum freedom, maximum harmony, maximum equality, and maximum sociability . . . what more is there to ask for? The prospect is so perfect that just about everybody wants to join the privacy bandwagon. "Privacy is good for you" is a rallying cry used by everyone, from bankers to the unemployed, from the top civil servant to the lowly office clerk, from the minister to his chauffeur. Dissonant voices are rare.

It is somewhat reminiscent of the ecological issue. Everyone considers the environment so important that no one in the economic, political, and administrative sector can afford to set up a project without adding a touch of green. We have eco-labels on consumer products, ecological priorities in political party programs, sponsorship of environment-friendly actions by notorious polluters, and, of course, a nauseating amount of lip service. But in the end, does it make the environment any better? Do any of these actions have a positive impact or are they for naught? In the end, will they be part of an environmental policy which will control complex problems or will they have the perverse effect of giving us a good conscience without even affecting the environmental problems as such? For example, does the "polluter pays" principle really result in a reduction of pollution? Or does it merely mean that the "payer" can continue to pollute, but with a clean conscience? How big is the gap between green talk and a green environment? Can capitalism and modern times change anything at all about their environmental policy? Or is pollution inherent to the system, and does the system have to be overthrown before something can change in the relation between nature and culture? The answers to these questions are never unequivocally positive or negative, even if radical ecologists may strongly disagree. Without a doubt, there is empty talk, perverse effects, bad faith. Pollution is and remains intimately intertwined with the global economic and political system. But does this mean there is no other way out than to accept defeat and wait for the green revolution which will abolish the free market and subjugate culture to what is called the "natural order"? Or are there realistic developments which deserve support? In the end, who dares to claim that in a quarter-century of environmental law and green policies nothing has changed? Would it not be a lot worse without protection? So even if a healthy dose of skepticism is called for, one has to try to exploit as much as possible the critical potential of the politico-environmental developments. If only for truly pragmatic reasons.

In fact, the same sort of skepticism applies to privacy. The arguments calling for an improved protection of privacy are so self-evident that there are very few naysayers. But is there more to this than meets the eye? Do we really enjoy the freedom of privacy as told? Does the story give us practical tools to achieve this ideal? Or not even that? Is all of this just a mirage, or is there truly more privacy on the horizon?

There are good reasons to be skeptical. History shows that the concept of privacy is relatively new. The developments which allowed privacy to blossom are just as recent—the separation between things public and private; secularization; the waning of traditions, customs and family ties; the preeminence of the individual; the open and pluralist nature of the state; and the importance of the political minority. On the other hand, privacy is developing at a time when it can be reduced to very little. Never have there been so many ways to meddle with the individual and his or her privacy, and never have there been so many ways to invade privacy as over the past century. Invasions of individual privacy are as recent as the protection of individual privacy. This is cause for concern since we have to interpret a discourse which, from the start, has coincided with practices running counter to it. How can the two be reconciled? In the end, laws protecting the privacy of telecommunication always turn out to be laws which, in certain cases, allow for wiretapping and taping. So is the privacy reasoning just an empty shell in which privacy can be reduced to as little as nothing? How do the noble and lofty privacy laws function in social reality? Can they affect anything?

In law, too, two narratives run side by side, and one certainly does not bring us the same emancipatory message as the other. Privacy as a collection of subjective rights is not the same as privacy as individual freedom. The former is paternalistic and moralizing. By pinpointing what belongs to the right of privacy and what doesn't, it limits the freedom of privacy rather than protects it (e.g., the *Hardwick* case mentioned in chapter 1). It comes down to the fact that the justification for the violation of privacy will be judged in light of the actions it uncovered. Filming or taking pictures of an individual without consent is a violation of the personality right covering depictions. But if this course of action leads to the discovery of an error or a crime—e.g., an employee smokes on the toilet during working hours—it would justify the violation of privacy. The end justifies the means, even if the latter violate a basic right. From this point of view, the basic right only grants protection to normal, conscientious, and everyday behavior. Additionally, the theory of personality rights gives it an absolute nature. Their violation would automatically yield an illegal action. That way, the individual obtains a right to privacy which, in principle, can be enforced whatever the circumstances, elements, and context of the case. This way privacy loses its relational dimension and degenerates into a closed, "autistic" right.

Privacy claims are often associated with selfish and petty bourgeois individualism. It turns into the vector of the selfish individual. This is of course linked to privacy's patrician origins. S. D. Warren, L. D. Brandeis, and their "right to be let alone" represent a wealthy, smug, exclusive, and self-centered upper-crust life which abhors publicity and public space. The living conditions of others, though, have little to do with this. Their privacy concept represents an atomized and suspicious society where individuals are urged to be indifferent, isolated, autarkic, and lacking in solidarity. It protects the conniving citizen who takes care of his own interests without taking any public or societal dimension into account. There is no longer a relationship between individual freedom and a social project. This point of view turns privacy into an ultraliberal creed which will be used by an elite against the state and the authorities, as well as against other citizens. Instead of protecting the freedom of self-determination, which spawns the participation of everyone in the public sphere, it backs the withdrawal into the private sphere and increases the suspicion of all legal and political institutions. Such privacy is the expression of a hypocritical and elitist culture instead of a tolerant and pluralist one. Emancipation has no place in this. To use a Marxist expression: privacy is an illusion. It creates a false consciousness and only aids and abets petty bourgeois property individualism.

Privacy in a Capitalist Market Economy:
A Contradiction in Terms?

The assertions in the previous paragraphs are supported by sound economic arguments. In truth, what can privacy mean without the necessary social and material conditions? What does privacy mean to the homeless and the unemployed? Probably as much as fundamental rights and freedoms mean to a sick, starving African, a pariah in India, or street children in South America. It means little to nothing. Is there a point to privacy if people do not have the means or power to enjoy freedom? To put it in more practical terms: What does the inviolability of the home mean to the homeless? No one can put into question that residents in luxury apartments and fancy neighborhoods and that owners of estates guarded by security systems and pit bulls have far better opportunities to protect their privacy than people living in decrepit neighborhoods, housing projects, or in one of the endless rows of apartment blocks. Privacy is for sale and goes to those with the funds to acquire decent housing. And since the best housing is reserved for a moneyed minority, it gives the common and universal principles of privacy and the inviolability of the home a hollow ring. Governments may have "positive obligations," but only up to a point. The question remains, however, To what extent does the state still control the free market which organizes the allocation of the means of production and subsistence?

Marxists have already pointed out the contradiction between the capitalist free-market economy and the claims to privacy. An ideally functioning self-regulating free market must also be a market where all participants have access to all relevant information to make the right decisions on their economic activities. The same applies to information on workers and consumers alike, since the best possible information on them needs to be gathered to reach the best possible transaction. So, as a rule of thumb, personal information is asked for, or even required, during job applications, requests for a bank loan, the establishment of insurance contracts, and so forth. The employer wants to know whether job applicants are qualified and have the right attitude, how the applicants performed at their previous jobs, whether drinking is a problem, whether they have AIDS, whether they are strongly religious, whether they are just married and might get pregnant soon, and whether they will be responsible for the rearing of the children, affecting their hours on the job. Before granting a loan or credit, a banker will want to know whether the client makes enough money, whether he or she lives frugally, how money is spent, and other information on the individual's personal life. A salesperson must be sure a client is creditworthy. A life insurance salesman wants to limit any risk and will inquire about the health and medical history of a prospective client. Homeowners look into the social habits and creditworthiness of potential tenants. The list goes on and all these examples have one common denominator: the lopsided balance of power forcing the weak party to surrender information. The banker and insurance salesman do not have to shed any personal information. It is one-way traffic forcing the weak party, either legally, contractually, or out of sheer need, to surrender privacy. Economic clout and financial independence appear to be privacy's best safeguards. A wealthy individual living off his investments in a castle has privacy.

As a result, the free market abhors privacy. The legal recognition of privacy counters the free market's principle of transparency. It is thus hardly surprising that Richard Posner, the ultraliberal guru of the "law and economics" movement, considers the protection of privacy as a gross distortion of the free market. It allows individuals to misrepresent themselves in an attempt to manipulate the market. What's more, privacy is increasing the cost of trade, thus affecting everyone.

So in a strange twist of political analysis, Marxists and ultraliberals fully agree in considering privacy incompatible with the capitalist free-market economy. The ultraliberals want to reduce privacy legislation, just like they want to cut back on any government interference. Those who want privacy will have to earn it on the market. Those who consider their privacy has been affected by market forces are free to go look elsewhere. It is the usual cynicism, putting "market laws" ahead of human beings. Marxists argue that the discrepancy between the prerogatives of the market and the privacy issue highlights an impasse. A society which embraces capitalism cannot possibly guarantee privacy since a great number of violations of privacy are inherent to capitalist economic practice. The history of privacy proves this amply and this is also in evidence in everyday reality. And since it can be established that a fundamental value like privacy cannot prevail over general and competing conduct, one evidently has to conclude that privacy is "pure ideology."

For Marxists, the concept of privacy is useless. Each action to boost privacy obfuscates and reinforces the system, which, in fact, invades privacy. The privacy claim contains no emancipatory potential. So where do we go from here? What can be done? As so often with Marxist legal theoretical analysis, the power of the argument is inversely proportional to the solutions being offered. The perversion of the democratic constitutional state's freedom and equality by the economic forces and capitalism is the subject of precise and straightforward argumentation. The same goes for the inevitable erosion of privacy. But how all this should be countered remains a mystery. Fight for the demise of capitalism? Revolt or wait for the revolution to happen? Today's prospects are quite something! Move to where life is better? But where is that exactly? Should we take one last, deep sigh and commit suicide? Should we withdraw from society and set up a personal network of friends, eat and debate together, prepare the next ideological conflict, and smoke a joint . . . while cocooning in the warm embrace of Western privacy?

The Welfare State and Privacy: Another Contradiction in Terms?

Or perhaps there is a hope that the state can counter the excesses of the market and create a privacy surplus. This hope, however, is diminishing by the day because capitalism and the free market have become a global force backed by a pervasive and performing communication technology. The state is losing its grip on the economy, and nowadays, its power has been replaced by the clout of the market. The political program of the welfare state and society was to control and correct the market, and this is now in decline. The goal was to fulfill the social economic human rights—provide social security, labor, health care, housing, education, security, leisure, welfare, et cetera. To counter insecurity, risks, and the inhuman self-regulation of the free market, the welfare state wanted to safeguard minimum standards of living for everyone, whatever his or her importance within the market system.

Economic capitalism interacts this way with interventionist social policy. Solidarity is organized for those who fall through the free market's safety net. In essence, it centers on redistribution without affecting the market principle. The authorities provide support for the jobless, the homeless, the poor, the sick, the handicapped, pensioners, large families, widows, and victims of occupational diseases and industrial accidents, and everyone is insured against any incident which undermines his or her market value. But does this system also contribute to the protection of privacy and personal freedom? No, it doesn't. To the contrary, support depends on an individual's right to it and to prove this, personal transparency is called for. The extent of support depends on the extent of available personal information. The welfare and social security systems both invade the realm of privacy. In this they differ little from those powerful market forces. Marxist analysts consider this only self-evident since the welfare state is foremost a capitalist instrument which has inherited the free-market logic.

Another factor is the fact that the emergence of the welfare state coincides with a number of fundamental changes which affect privacy. The basic hands-off attitude of the liberal state is replaced by far-reaching and across-the-board government interference aimed at controlling and guiding individuals. Backed by social sciences, the idea of the "constructibility" of society takes central stage. After all, the best way to counter the adverse effects of the market is to prevent them. Prevention has to combat disorder, poverty, crime, social exclusion, and unfair social economic relations. Michel Foucault and François Ewald have shown that the welfare state, more than protecting everyone's freedom, tries to influence the behavior of individuals to reduce risks. As a result, the welfare sector, social security, equal opportunity programs, mandatory insurance systems, preventive medicine, and other social services work hard to identify risk groups and individuals. This management concept leads to an ever-deeper and more precocious, preventive, and productive interference in the lives of individuals. People become ever-more transparent and vulnerable, at the cost of privacy's freedom.

This search for symptoms (prevention) requires interference well beyond the sanctioning of infractions (repression). It also implies a view which not only identifies nonconformity, but also designates the needs and scope of services for society. Such a portrayal of mankind is no longer based on the free and unique individual, but on the average, normal individual, which social science has carefully put into statistical lists. The authorities use such categories as "dangerous" youths, "dangerous" mental patients, "dangerous" environments, incompetent parents, abnormal individuals, and similar terms. The normalization policy is based on the average individual in a normal social context. Freedom is a nuisance because it is unpredictable and elusive. Efficiency shoves privacy aside. Whatever the good intentions of the welfare state, it offers no solution, no alternative for privacy within the confines of the free market. In such a situation, privacy wanes.

Privacy's Emancipatory Potential

The analyses are anything but encouraging. If we take them as such, we are stuck. Twice, we strike a contradiction in terms because privacy seems totally incompatible with both the liberal capitalist state and the capitalist welfare state. Apparently, there is nothing to be done about that. The double con-tradiction turns each action or claim backing privacy into mere "ideology," mystification, hollow babbling. It reinforces a false consciousness—and thus backs capitalism and its welfare state.

Fortunately we don't have to accept the analyses lock, stock, and barrel. Marxist analysts have a tendency to write themselves into a corner. This fundamentally has to do with the impossibility to reinterpret revolutionary thought to fit a situation which is anything but revolutionary. Besides a handful of Maoists, no one in the West believes in the use, let alone the possibility, of a socialist revolution. It doesn't really matter whether this is bad news; for years now, the revolution has failed to mobilize the masses. What is disappointing is the fact that the sharp analyses, still composed with the intransigence of yore, invariably reach the conclusions of yore: the capitalist economy, the source of all abuses, has to be adapted or changed. The conclusions apply to both the global project of the democratic state and privacy in particular. The argument goes that in both cases the economic infrastructure allots power, keeping it out of the grasp of such suprastructural phenomena as law and politics. The democratic constitutional state: exit right. The welfare state: exit left. Exit human rights. Exit privacy. But what do we get instead? We get the Marxist author's joy to have made those points and a perplexed audience. Beyond any doubt, we get a number of valid points. What we don't get is even a hint of a credible and contemporary alternative.

The democratic constitutional state is deeply involved in the issue of power distribution, much more than most analysts want to acknowledge. It aims to keep the balance of power as much as possible within an acceptable proportionality, taking more into account than just economic clout. Differ-ent constitutional powers establish a balance which is kept in check by the people and the media. The balance of power between individuals and/or legal entities is just as much the subject of legal assessment. Citizens have their prerogatives, which they can enforce with sharply varying measures of success. Some powerful economic forces, though, always seem to get their way. Of course, states find it tougher and tougher to get a grip on interna-tional capitalism. Life is good in the West because the international econ-omy exports misery elsewhere. But at least the democratic constitutional state is a project which takes the real distribution of power into account. As a project it has more credibility than "suppression of capitalism," or the bizarre belief that a dictatorship will voluntarily abolish itself to create a society without a power structure.

Even if the democratic state has clear weaknesses and even if a lot of ideals get lost in practice, it still remains the most realistic and the most desirable model of society. Instead of radically dismissing the present, it is essential to interpret its emancipatory dimension, but not without taking the criticism into account. Human rights and the rule of law must be the unambiguous point of departure. They are obfuscating insofar as they shroud the power relations and the inequalities. But at the same time, they are a major achievement since they are emancipatory, both politically and judicially. The latter is undeniably the case if they guarantee the autonomy, freedom, and self-determination of an individual and if they protect an individual against the ambitions of the authorities, legal entities, and other citizens. Privacy does indeed have an emancipatory dimension.

And this is evident from the opposite side in the fact that all totalitarian projects abolish the concept of privacy. Brutal totalitarian regimes such as Nazism and Stalinism abolished all privacy protection. Controls, discrimination based on identity, wiretapping, spying, opening letters, arbitrary searches, torture, and deportations, were common. It is also noteworthy that disciplinary total institutions, including prisons, boarding schools, and asylums, practically eliminate privacy too. For anyone with remaining doubts, just watch Stanley Kubrick's *Full Metal Jacket*. Literature also has plenty of examples—Franz Kafka's *The Trial*, Aldous Huxley's *Brave New World*, Anthony Burgess's *A Clockwork Orange*, George Orwell's *1984*, and le Marquis de Sade's *120 Days of Sodom*. They all are eye-catching fictional examples of the unmistakable link between totalitarian power and the liquidation of privacy. These examples are still sufficiently bearable to read since they are sufficiently fictional. However, this changes when we turn to the elimination of privacy in such autobiographic novels as Fyodor Dostoyevsky's *The House of the Dead*. It becomes unbearable when we turn to realistic camp literature. The destruction of privacy truly is an instrument of power. Privacy is a thorn in the side of those who seek more or absolute power.

This turns the role of privacy as a claim to freedom into something essential. As Michel Foucault (in Dreyfus and Rabinow 1984) wrote, all power relationships presuppose a tension between the behavior, itself the product of power, and the resistance it creates. Power as a behavioral conduit—*une conduite des conduites*—always implies a moment of resistance, namely the moment when individuals consider behavioral alternatives. At this stage, all human relations are marked, one way or another, by power. This is certainly so when power is defined as the relation between individuals, when one steers the behavior of the other, even though the other has the freedom to act differently. Power is a strategic situation that produces behavior in an individual which he or she would not commit to spontaneously. Resistance is always at the heart of the balance of power. That balance is never settled and the tension it embodies remains at stake. Each power relationship is determined by the resistance it generates. It is at this elementary level where privacy comes in, since personal freedom embodies all possible behavioral alternatives, including, per definition, resistance to power. In other words, privacy is the recognition of the resistance which has to face up to power itself. The constitutional democratic state sets out to quash any absolute balance of power, which after all it already did to the absolute monarchy, again proving privacy's essential role in such a state.

Privacy imposes a balancing of power and resistance in all power relationships. And this does not only apply to the interference of companies and the welfare state. The list also includes, if necessary, family morals, trade unions, police, doctors, scientists, et cetera. The legal system is full of examples—some successful, some not—of attempts to safeguard the privacy of individuals by protecting it against powerful interests. Police services cannot invade the privacy of a home at will. Welfare workers also have to operate within limits. Homeowners do not have the unlimited right, despite the absolute right to property, to check on their tenants. Employers cannot check on their personnel and their telecommunication exchanges at will. Banks and insurance companies are, in principle, limited in their freedom to gather, process, and pass on personal information. The Strasbourg Court has forced plenty of states to adapt its legislation. So privacy does function in a legal system, even if the end result is often limited and disappointing. But there is nothing to stop anyone from bolstering and radicalizing the claim for more privacy.

Overall, this is a plea to underpin the emancipatory side of privacy and increase and radicalize its impact. Thus, it remains necessary to put the real power relations into perspective and not assume that everyone has the same social and economic possibilities. The lopsided reality of horizontal private relations is such that the privacy of the weak party is often under threat. Insurance contracts, loans, and rental agreements illustrate how the weak party is rendered transparent. It is no different when it comes to the authorities. The impact of privacy has to increase most in such relationships, if it is to have any impact at all. A rule of thumb could be "the bigger the imbalance of power, the bigger the protection of privacy." For example, the consent of an individual should not always be considered a legal justification to invade privacy, since this person may not have a choice.

It is just as important to keep on stressing the freedom aspect of privacy. "Never tell what the content of privacy is" could be another rule of thumb. Indeed, for reasons we have already mentioned, privacy should not be described as a "right to" something because this approach backfires. Individual freedom has to remain key. It doesn't matter what is normal, acceptable, or average, just as it doesn't matter what the individual is expected to be. Privacy is the freedom of self-determination. Add to that social and cultural diversity and plurality. All resulting behavior has to be automatically accepted as long as it does not clash with other legal norms. In that case, the judge has to consider the interests at stake and take the importance of privacy into account. If certain rules legitimize disproportionate attacks on freedom, the legislator has to adapt those rules.

The refusal to define the content of privacy also counters the threat of excess juridicization. The freedom of privacy does not need legal templates. Freedom can only flourish where force and meddling are absent. Personality rights achieve exactly the opposite: they import rules where freedom should reign. This is baneful. A right to friendship, for example, which implies what friendship has to be and should not be (defining what is not covered by that right), is probably the best way to undermine friendships.

Even though the critical potential of privacy freedom is stressed, this does not have to mean that the existing economic differences and material needs are disregarded. This is, after all, an old issue in human rights law. It comes down to the issue of the relation between the first and second generation of human rights, long a source of discord. The first generation, or the classic individual freedoms, seeks to limit the powers of the state, which should refrain from interference. The second generation, or the social, economic, and cultural rights (the equality rights), seeks to improve the material well-being of individuals by imposing on the state positive duties and interventions. The first generation guarantees the full enjoyment of such freedoms as speech, association, and privacy. The second generation asks for state intervention to achieve material wealth, social and cultural equality, and the principle of equal opportunity. Any question on the relation between the two has a "chicken or the egg" quality about it. Without freedom, there is no material wealth. Without material wealth, there is no freedom. The second generation was more important in the Eastern bloc countries, while the West preferred the first generation. The rest of the world had no say in this since they basically were colonies. The East bloc never included freedom and suffered the consequences of terror and demagoguery of the leaders, disinterest and resignation on the part of the population, black markets and parallel economies . . . all leading to total disintegration. It is still evident in many former Eastern bloc nations how little freedom means without material wealth. The West had its freedom, but applied it selectively to the colonial populations, women at home, minorities, African Americans in the United States, who all had little or even less. Since World War II, socioeconomic and cultural equality has made great inroads, especially during the Golden Sixties. Yet, inequality remains and is even increasing again.

There is a self-evident link between material and cultural wealth and the possibility to enjoy freedom and privacy. We are not going to claim that the West offers equal opportunities to all. To the contrary, problems and dodgy policy are not in short supply. But it is probably too much to expect that progress is made across the board. Human rights constitute one whole and if everything cannot be achieved at once, all dimensions have to be and remain an integral part of the project. It means that more effort has to go into the creation of equal opportunities in the socioeconomic and cultural fields. Privacy can probably be useful to back up this line of reasoning. Freedom can only be achieved under certain material conditions, and it will vary strongly from individual to individual. Some may enjoy their freedom on the road and reject any help because of this. But they are hardly representative of society as a whole. Nevertheless, they must at least have been offered the opportunity to set out on a different course.

Privacy cannot be perfectly meshed into the economic process of society. Privacy's discourse can also be extremely moralizing and a symbol of selfish individualism. It can also create expectations that can never be met. Even with this skeptical thought in mind, there is enough reason to believe that privacy can have a truly emancipatory impact. In this case, instead of stressing the repressive and obfuscating component of the privacy issue, freedom, autonomy, and self-determination come to the fore. It renders the emancipatory potential of the privacy claim explicit. At the heart of the issue is individual freedom, and more precisely, the right of everyone to resist when one's behavior is steered or subjected to power. This component of privacy needs to be reinforced and radicalized. The next two chapters highlight this. Chapter 4 discusses a number of dangers which have not been mentioned up to now and which seriously threaten individual freedom, necessitating the protection of resistance. In chapter 5, the issue of information processing is seen as a typical example of privacy's ambiguity.

CHAPTER FOUR

Privacy Endangered

The Techno-scientific Developments and the Myths They Spawn

We have often referred to the impact of technical developments on privacy, and computer science has figured prominently. Information technology has enabled the lightning-fast, efficient, delocalized, and omnipresent processing of enormous amounts of personal information. It has made individuals and their behavior transparent, retraceable, and controllable, which seriously curtails privacy. This trend was already ongoing and is not linked to progress in computer science per se. Information technology, however, added two new components. The first centers on the obvious technical advances: the gigantic increase in information processing capacity and the potential to converge the different existing methods of information processing. Sound, vision, movement, smell, materials—everything can be digitalized. This increases and diversifies the threat to privacy. In essence, every individual trace can be linked to all others. This and the subsequent sections will take a closer look at technological developments.

The second dimension is different. It centers on the discursive universe within which information technology develops. The 1970s were swamped with stories and theories claiming that a new era was dawning and that the West was going through a fundamental and decisive (r)evolution. The intellectual universe and many a bookshop were creaking under the weight of such titles as *The Coming of Post-industrial Society* (Bell), *The Coming Infor-*

mation Age (Dizard), *The Information Society as Post-industrial Society* (Masuda), *L'informatisation de la société* (Nora and Minc), *La société digitale* (Mercier, Plassard, and Scardigli), *De informatiemaatschappij* (Uitgave 50 jaar Natuur en Techniek), *The Wired Society* (Martin), *The Third Wave* (Toeffler), *The Micro Revolution* (Laurie), *The Micro-Electronics Revolution* (Forester), and *The Mighty Micro* (Evans). New words and concepts emerged: electronic age, knowledge society, compunications, technotronic society, the communications revolution, computopia, l'univers informationnel, mediapolis, technopolis, global village, et cetera, ad infinitum. Glossing over the subtle differences among all these concepts and stories, one thing is clear—they all brought the same happy message: information technology is fundamentally changing society since "information" as an economic and social factor was taking center stage.

For these writers, the 1970s opened a third phase in history. Phase one was the preindustrial society which was economically centered on fishing, agriculture, and mining. Land property was the major economic and social-political factor. Society has gone well beyond this, but phase two—industrial society with its means of production, goods, energy, and money as key characteristics—is also quickly fading. It leaves us in phase three—postindustrial society with information, computer science, and telecommunication as its predominant components. This new society runneth over with promise. It legitimizes the great expectations, since the surplus knowledge of society and the incredible growth of information are bound to create a better world. A vast majority of the predictions claim that the drastic changes will put an end to the capitalist means of production, will ensure political participation in a decentralized process of decision making, will increase cultural and creative development . . . the rosy visions go on and on. To quote Yoneji Masuda: a "computopia on earth" is within reach and its historic monument will be "only several chips one inch square in a small box."

Hence, the introduction of information technology into society was accompanied by a loud and omnipresent legitimacy story. Technological developments were presented as the next step in the relentless development of mankind. This next step held countless promises of economic, social, political, and cultural betterment. Improved and fair, more efficient and democratic: the future looked bright. One had to be mad to protest and initially only a tiny minority offered some resistance. A number of doom scenarios questioned the ideology and the promises of the information society (Schiller, Roszak, Hamelink, Ellul, Winner), without much success. Information technology was unleashed on society at an ever-faster pace. Even now, information technology companies and computer giants are competitively forced to upgrade their product line, leaving hapless consumers wondering why their two-year-old computer is no longer powerful enough, cannot read some suddenly vital computer card, and, worst of all, is no longer compatible.

Pretty fast, it became evident that this fundamentally changed and improved world was little more than a mirage. There are precious few indications of substantial changes in the balance of power between individuals, between citizens and the state, between big business and the working class, let alone between the West and the developing world. Even the most anticipated expectation, that information technology would facilitate access to information and thus make things better, has not been met. Policy and power became more opaque and harder to grasp, a far cry from the promise of greater transparency. The "postvisionary" stories were soon exposed as myths. People still don't eat information, they still cannot buy things by telling the cashier a story and "transmitting information," they have not changed their participation in political decision making. There is just as much exploitation, destruction, and warfare. The frog that wanted to inflate itself into an oxen just turned into a big frog.

The "information society" has been glorified as "electronic Eden on earth" (Dizard), yet it is nothing else than a highly performing technological, industrial, and trade society in which information technology contributes to achieve higher efficiency and even corners part of the market itself. Introducing computers in the production and service sectors has proved highly profitable in economic terms. At a political level, information technology has made control over decentralized activities easier. It has turned culture superficial and contributed to the establishment of a monoculture. It has provided both excess information and disinformation. On top of that, information technology has perpetuated and saved institutions which would have been faced with an incapacity to keep up with the need for ever-more information processing (administration, banking, social security, the military establishment, et cetera). The levelheaded comment of Joseph Weizenbaum, one of the pioneers of artificial intelligence no less, was: "Yes, the computer came right on time. But on time for what? On time to maintain, buttress, and stabilize social and political structures which would otherwise have undergone radical renewal or succumbed under the weight of the demands that surely would have come."[1] So there was no Big Shift, but a reinforcement of the existing order.

Little wonder that the information technology conglomerate gets along just fine with the central figures of new capitalism. It reinforces their strategies. The functionality, accuracy, and efficiency of computers predestines them to reinforce the powers that be in a society which is driven by the same values. Computers meet the criteria of centralization, rationalization, professionalization, competitivity, operability, tradability, accuracy, functionality, and speed—all standards held in high esteem in business, the military, media, politics, research and development, and management "sciences." The result is the smooth transition from information technology to capitalism. Stanley Cohen (1985) put it forcibly: "Not a new social order, but more of the same."

This information society myth has had a strong, and negative, impact on the privacy debate. Law and privacy have been put on the defensive by information technology with its promises of progress and fundamental social change. What's more, information technology became the embodiment of the inevitability of so-called neutral techno-scientific progress. It immediately drew the battle lines. According to this line of thought, law had to adapt to techno-scientific development, not the other way around. A new society needed new laws. The legal system was expected to do its utmost to pave the way for "computopia" and its miracle products. It had to become the system's rainmaker.

And thus it was. "Computer law" was born and is still spawning research centers and information technology lawyers who, often backed by private-sector sponsors, join the chorus which wants law to adapt to information technology and technological developments. Suddenly, gone is the legendary meticulousness of legal experts, and overnight they turn into the swift and happy messengers of the inescapable new reality. They further erode law in their haste to turn it into a subservient and subordinate accomplice of the inevitable future. Computer law has given birth to countless legal absurdities, including "theft of information," copyright protection of computer programs, and also the ambiguous privacy legislation centering on information technology (more about this in the final section). "Information technology law" usually fails to maintain any autonomy and falls over itself just to be able to keep up with the information technology wave and abet developments.

Techno-scientific developments, however, are never inevitable, never neutral. Sociology of sciences has shown that they always are the product of a human project and the work of a network of scientists, research leaders, companies, sponsors, politicians, investors, institutions, and so forth. These networks make deliberate choices, make decisions, and take irreversible steps. Any "end product" for an "end user" has gone through a list of small and major decisions that have molded the product and led to its final commercialization. Hence, the development of information technology is the result of micropolitics in action. It is preeminently sociopolitical. This intrinsic political aspect, however, is shrouded in the myths of techno-scientific neutrality and inevitability. And this contributes in a less-than-innocent way to the withdrawal of these activities from the social decision-making processes, be they political or legal.

It is also a fact that the skills humankind has developed are never limited to a single meaning and are always redefined by their users. A technological development has never once defined the future. Products are used, abused, and applied in myriad projects, continuously redefining their future. Humanity does not live beyond technology; the two are not opposed. Humanity is part of technology and gives it direction. Technology is closely linked to social organization, cultural values, institutions, social imagination, decisions, and controversies. The denial of this blocks the road toward a political, democratic, collective, and legal assessment of technology development. There is a high need to extend the sway of the democratic constitutional state to include techno-scientific production. This production should not be considered as inevitable neutral progress or irrefutable scientific fact. No, "technodemocracy," to use Pierre Levy's term, is only conceivable when the technological phenomenon becomes part of culture and is considered a politico–legal experience.

Privacy remains essential, even in the face of techno-scientific developments which are presented as the inevitable fruit of progress, as if they are neutral and apolitical, beyond assessment, beyond doubt. There is no reason to adapt or weaken privacy's freedom just based on such stories. Law should not be sucked into the slipstream of techno-scientific developments. It would only lose its singularity. Law has to mediate, also in conflicts of interests relating to information technology. There is a need for balance and both privacy and the public interest should be able to throw their full weight into the scales of Justice. Legislation and case law should both be on a quest to find such balance.

Of course, all this does not only apply to information technology; it also applies to all other products of the techno-scientific networks. They too are the result of projects and micropolitical decision making. They, too, are debatable truth claims and certainly not the incontestable truth. Their obvious "non-neutrality," however, does not mean they should be rejected out of hand. Beware, this book is not a technophobic or antiscientific pamphlet. We don't want to go back in time. What is at stake is using the available knowledge and means to question both the obvious and hidden impact of our high-technological society. Insofar as they are the fruit of human labor, all techno-scientific artifacts should evidently be brought within the scope of human judgment.

This only increases the importance of privacy's freedom, since countless techno-scientific developments can have an impact on the personal freedom of individuals. Public space is constantly being filled with products full of meanings, space–time conceptions, and mental views which can limit and stupefy the freedom of action and even thought. These products have widely varying origins. Personal freedom can be influenced by medical and genetic progress, just as it can be by new materials or construction techniques. Privacy then becomes an essential touchstone which allows citizens to take legal steps when they feel that a certain techno-scientific development erodes or threatens a personal freedom. As such, privacy can be an expression of resistance. The legal system has to take this privacy claim and privacy's interest very seriously and not be affected by stories on the inevitability of progress that counter privacy. Personal freedom carries a lot of weight and illegitimate steering of behavior should be banned. Nothing is inevitable, nothing is fateful, nothing is exclusively "progress." There are always people, there are always "culprits." Law should not bend to the superhuman and inevitable patterns of postvisionary and epistemological stories. In the next section, we investigate whether the "privacy legislations" which came into force to streamline personal information processing meet the legal terms of reference. Do they allow citizens to resist the personal information processors? Or are they nothing more than shiny legal wrapping to confirm the fait accompli of generalized personal information processing?

Social Science Profiles and Normalization

The impact of the representation of man created by modern social science constitutes a second danger threatening privacy. Social science creates profiles, "pigeonholes," and statistical averages which allow for the measurement of normal behavior. Instead of highlighting individual specifics, they refer to the greatest common denominator and the average of the group (and more general, society, humanity). The free and independent individual and all its uniqueness are shoved aside for the exact opposite: the serial model lacking any distinctive trait, Mr. and Mrs. Average. These models are in ample supply, even in daily life. The model student, the good parent, the perfect employee, the balanced rational individual, normal (missionary position) sex, a normal life, and good health are but a few examples of profiles which have both a trivial and scientific impact. Juxtaposed are a series of negative profiles, and they often give cause to a series of invasions of privacy: the bad pupil, the stubborn student, the negligent parent, the endangered child, the problem child, the young delinquent, the hysterical woman, the psychic case, the hyperventilating individual, the madman, the psychopath, the common criminal, the kleptomaniac, and a whole series of sexual deviants, much the target of giggles, including onanists, ephebophiles, fetishists, bestiality lovers, necrophiliacs.

Scientific and trivialized labels are used as reference and soundboard for countless social decisions. Somebody whose behavior does not fit the normal, average mold stands out. That person is at risk of falling by the wayside, sometimes with tragic consequences. Someone who is considered insane is at risk of being locked up; someone who acts "abnormally" cannot find a job; negligent parents who stray from the pedagogic ideal lose custody over their children; a teacher who shows too much affection for his or her pupils risks losing his or her job (and worse) because he or she is considered a dangerous pedophile; until recently, vagrants could be jailed, but now they receive "support"; job selections are based on the ideal profile; and someone who steals merchandise in a shop four times is considered a dangerous kleptomaniac. All this while speedsters, tax evaders, or polluters are not considered "abnormal," "sick," or "dangerous". With bated breath, we still wait for such psycho-psychiatric inventions like "speedochism," "fraudophilia," and "pollutomania". But that's a different story.

Profiles do have serious social consequences. If you don't want to lose out or be excluded, adapt. Normal behavior is called for and produced. Freedom is eroded, behavior is manipulated, and freedom of self-determination is limited. Once more, privacy's freedom is sent down a slippery slope.

Michel Foucault has always stressed the fact that, from the start, legal–political enlightenment was accompanied by practices that countered it. The legal discourse of fundamental rights and freedoms faced social mechanisms which undermined it. These mechanisms consist of practices which seek to impose a normalization and disciplining of behavior, and they are backed by social sciences which legitimize the practices. Surveillance is observation and vice versa. Psychology and psychiatry develop out of the interaction with asylums; criminology and forensic behavioral sciences develop in prisons. The cradle of pedagogy is nineteenth-century institutional education. Knowledge and power are intertwined: it is the point of departure. There is no knowledge without power and no power without knowledge.[2]

The situation is ambiguous. The constitutional state guarantees an egalitarian system of rights and freedoms, but a series of power mechanisms erodes this. The "disciplines" and normalization are, according to Foucault, active throughout the social field and contribute to the erosion of legal freedoms. Who doesn't remember the effect of disciplinary action in the armed forces, school, the work floor, hospitals, within a family, and so on. A physical order where each individual is allotted a single space (the best pupil gets the front seat, each child/family member gets a room); a detailed time schedule (timetables, day schedules); a prescribed development in different phases (classes in school); a permanent hierarchal observation (supervised supervisors); normalizing sanctions which are presumed to be corrective and therapeutic (army drills, school punishments); examination and other tests which allow differentiation and sanctioning. Together, all these power procedures create an area within which the difference between normal and abnormal becomes visible. This happens within a framework of a norm which is sheer balance and comparison, without any reference as such to the individual. Foucault calls it a panoptic exercise of power: everybody is always visible and comparable much as it is in Bentham's Panopticon.

Social sciences operate in this area and have thrived there since the nineteenth century. Their development interacts with "disciplinarization" and vice versa. This is why the social sciences order, classify, arrange, and set averages. Statistics (the Quételet way) are their major ally. A cross section can be shown as a Gauss curve. A delinquent, for example, is an imprisoned individualized and categorized person promoted to the object of knowledge by criminologists. Only then does the delinquent have a "real" existence. The "psychiatric case" is held in an asylum because of the disorder that he or she created and is subsequently catalogued as such by psychiatrists. The social sciences live in correlation with a power system which isolates its subject (man, patients, the insane, the delinquent, the pervert, and so on). They are always tied to the power system within which they emerged. They have an important role to play in the active and passive normalization of the behavior of the free, equal and brotherly citizen living in contemporary society. It is the reason why Foucault writes that nowadays, it is more important to reject what we are than to discover what we are.[3]

So even if man is in principle free, his behavior is limited and affected by outside influences. The legal vision of the self-determining and free subject is countered by the production of normal, controlled and enforced behavior. Foucault is clear: the disciplines and their techniques are neither an extension or a base of law; they are incompatible with it. As a result, the West created a global regime which functions on two levels. On the one hand, the Enlightenment and its individual rights and freedoms still hold sway. This is countered, on the other hand, by obfuscating power mechanisms which are legitimized by the truth claims of the social sciences. The optimistic views of the Enlightenment create individuals full of initiative who are convinced their lives are theirs to live. But instead, daily discipline systematically normalizes them and limits their possibilities in life. As a result, Western society is repressive and permissive at the same time.

We don't have to fully adopt Foucault's radical analyses to recognize their importance. It is enough to accept that social science's truth claims have a normalizing effect. It means that, like all other human ventures, they can be judged, politically and legally. Because of this, they become neither bad nor fake. They shed their "objective" aura and they can no longer function as truth beyond suspicion. There is nothing scandalous about that. It is, in fact, pretty good news.

It does imply that law should not become the vector of social sciences' truth claims, nor should law become an instrument of a policy turned scientific. The law has to maintain its protection of freedom even when individuals are confronted with scientifically based activities which limit this freedom. Enlightened law should not become the cover for disciplinary and normalizing practices. But does legal reality bear this out?

It is a fact that law often seeks inspiration in the social sciences. This is evident when assessing the references of countless laws, the shedding of authority to behavioral professionals, and their strong presence in many procedures. Juvenile law, family law, social security law, law covering the insane and the incompetent, and penal law, to give just a few examples, are ridden with social science jargon and often rely on psychiatrists, social assistants, psychologists, pedagogues, and criminologists, before, during, and after procedures. Law still comes to the fore as law, but it is stuffed with scientific truth claims which are intrinsically intertwined with power. An attempt to produce normalized, channeled, and statistically and scientifically naturalized behavior pervades the discourse of fundamental rights and freedoms. A strong line of thought based on the idea that society can be masterminded or managed prevails at the expense of law's emancipatory and critical function. Nothing seems to be left to stop the invasion of the individual. Diversity is turned into uniformity. The aim is for predictability and transparency where freedom and noninterference should reign. The kaleidoscope of freedom is overshadowed by the gloom of normalcy.

It immediately shows how crucial the intransigent maintenance of privacy really is. Any resistance against normalization is first a show of personality. Not everyone wants to become Mr. or Mrs. Average; many would rather be themselves. Privacy is not only the legal way to show resistance but also an opportunity for law to regain its lost authenticity. This is why privacy should not turn into a cover for the further normalization of society. To put it in other terms, erosion also threatens privacy. That much was evident in the approach of privacy as a subjective right. One needs to rely on the normality criteria which were imported from either social sciences, ethics, or a combination of both to get to the heart of subjective law. It is very different from law applied through law. The possibility to mediate is reduced, or even disappears. Obfuscation and "false consciousness" become imminent.

Only a radical interpretation of privacy as personal freedom can be an effective point of departure for individual resistance against suffocating models. Since the truth claims of the social sciences can never be absolute—however useful, accurate, and well intentioned they may be—law must be able to offset them with the expressions of personal freedom and "other narratives." Privacy implies that an individual who has been declared insane by professionals can appeal and defend his or her case. These claims should not be swept aside by such arguments as "all mad people say they are not insane. This just proves insanity." Privacy implies that discrimination based on any departure from average behavior is outlawed or should at least be part of a legal process of balancing of interests. Privacy implies that the use of ideal profiles is limited. It also suggests that suspects in a court case are allowed to give their side of the story and receive a measure of protection from crime fighting, even if this has been rendered scientific. No matter how difficult it is to fathom "the other side," it is exactly there where room is available to develop the freedom of self-determination and the freedom to establish a distinct personality which may be atypical.

Europeans willing to resist the laws which impose an excessive amount of normalization and limit personal freedom can take their case to the European Court of Human Rights in Strasbourg. An individual who cannot enjoy freedom of privacy without fear of discrimination or administrative or legal sanctioning (if the sanction cannot be legitimized under the conditions of Article 8, paragraph 2 of the ECHR) can successfully challenge, as, for example, *Dudgeon* (1981) and *Norris* (1988) have proved. A judge too can invoke privacy to back up the freedom to be different. At stake is nothing less than an essential cornerstone of society—personal freedom and the freedom to be oneself without any unfounded interference from others. Leaning heavily on privacy, law has to guarantee maximum freedom, even in the face of the truth claims from the social sciences. As such, these truth claims and the power they represent are not the problem. Social science research gives us better insight into our own nature. After all, control also means understanding. Power as such has nothing despicable but it is omnipresent. It is part of our lives. But this is only possible if it can be countered, if resistance is recognized, and if law can always mediate between the powers that be. Privacy is important because it can shelter resistance and diversity.

Controlling Societies

The disciplines and the attached power mechanisms are strongly intertwined with such institutions as schools, the armed forces, factories, hospitals, asylums, and prisons. These institutions developed during the nineteenth century and reached their apex during the early twentieth century. At that stage, the individual was taken by the hand from one closed institution to the next. This analysis has to be updated, though, because of a series of interesting changes that have swept through the institutions since. Much has to do with the development of new and more subtle control techniques which allow a more effective steering of behavior, no longer through closed institutions, but in the open social field as such. Taking a cue from Foucault, this development was further explained and catalogued by Stanley Cohen, Gary Marx, and Gilles Deleuze. These authors expose the creeping erosion of our freedoms as a result of the development of a controlling and surveillance society. Gary Marx and Gilles Deleuze respectively claim we live in a "maximum security society" or in a *société de contrôle* which relies on a refined technological framework to influence, even "program" the daily lives of citizens. Interaction forces social sciences into similar changes, extending the link between power and knowledge.

The reforms of the medical institutions, the psychiatric wards, prisons, education, and industry are at the heart of our exposé. They all progressively adapt to the devalorization of the closed institution, the new expectations, an increased social mobility, and the faster pace of life. At the same time, they widen their radius and improve performance. Continued, discreet controls in the open reinforce the cumbersome and slow methods. The former disciplines were novel, yet analogue, molds in which the individual was forced to start again constantly, and was again submitted to hierarchal observation, normalizing judgment, examination, and pacification. On the other hand, the controls continue much more as contextualized modulations or as molds which constantly adapt themselves to the setting. When it comes to the desired impact, the new control mechanism can rival the disciplinary incarcerations. They normalize and streamline behavior just as much. Nevertheless, they allow the individual to continue to live within society, or "float" within society, as Deleuze puts it. Currently, the management becomes more complete in the sense that the molds interlock, which eventually leads to the channeling of flows of individuals.

A case in point is the expansion of the closed hospital system with an elaborate network of ambulant health care in which the patient or "careseeker" increases freedom of movement. Yet that movement will be painstakingly checked by social aid workers, psychologists, psychiatrists, and even police officials in their capacity as service providers. The most important impact of this development likely is the generalization of control. The number of beds and rooms in a hospital is limited while the social care network, pushing the limits of the ill-defined sector, peers into the smallest nooks and crannies of social life. Health and disease are subjected to permanent management, spurred on by an ever-wider variety of consumer-friendly medical drugs. This movement is also encouraged in the medical sciences. Ambulant care is considered more effective than institutional care. The family doctor becomes the gatekeeper between the two systems.

Or consider for that matter the classic capitalist factory, which aims to increase production as much as possible at the lowest possible cost of labor. Workers have been individualized based on their function within the company and everyone has a physical, functional, and hierarchical position within the system. Changes, such as promotions, are exceptional and do not have a major impact. The best strategy is to keep a low profile. The best worker is the "useful idiot": maximum physical energy, minimal mental resistance. Contemporary companies, though, are much more flexible and promote a far greater individual mobility. Everyone should be flexible. Short-term management has become an instrument of social control. The pay scale is no longer exclusively linked to a position within a company but has been largely individualized. Competitions, matches, challenges, company presents and gadgets, and jobs groaning under the weight of an official title (assistant communication manager for a gofer) are just some of the tricks employers use to boost production. Nowadays, companies have much-publicized "philosophies" (Deleuze calls this *la nouvelle la plus terrifiante du monde*) which have to motivate workers and influence behavior. Everyone is expected to make the objectives of the company his or her own.

The same development can also be seen within the prison system. An increasing array of alternatives has complemented the prison institution as

such, however, without solving the problem of overcrowding. Electronic surveillance provides a convict with an electronic leash which limits his radius
of movement and transmits his location. A lot of "alternative sanctions"
allow convicts to stay outside the prison walls. Release on parole is almost
always conditional and, as a result, increases surveillance: mandatory report-
ing, exclusion from certain areas, psychosocial forensic counseling, mandatory medication, et cetera. Checks on someone's presence quickly turn into
movement surveillance. But the shadow of a prison building still functions
as a deterrent.

At school, too, exposure increases. Education used to be limited to well-
defined periods and institutions. Now, it spills over, in time and space. Correspondence and computers allow people to get an education at home. Education has also become interminable with the availability of ever more
specialization, additional training, and evening courses. Furthermore, Deleuze claims that education will shed ever more of its closed features and
merge with the professional world. Continued professional formation, and
the ensuing competitive spirit, become part of the company culture. If one
wants to make more money, one has to study more; and there is an endless
array of master's degrees and postgraduates to continue the process of "self-
realization." Education becomes never-ending. This new situation is evident
in the development of universities as ill-defined institutions that have to
redefine themselves constantly to meet financial, ideological, and political
expectations. Universities align themselves ever closer with companies.
Broad social education is wiped off the board by professional training. Fundamental research loses out to product-related research. Private sponsorship
has to be wooed, since the authorities are becoming stingy.

Control is expanded without the loss of the disciplinary institutions. A
continuum emerges and spreads well beyond the closed institutions. Stanley
Cohen (1985) said that the net is cast wider and the mesh size is getting
smaller. An increasing number of individuals is submitted to the system
(wider nets). The interventions are intensified (denser nets). And the number of actors outside of the traditional institutions is also increasing (different
nets). At the same time, the outlying frontiers of the control system are
getting fuzzier. They have become totally opaque at the inside and outside of
the framework. The spread of the integrated and integrating control mechanism in the social area seems unlimited. The borderline between the public
and private interventions is also getting less distinct. We have private police
forces, the prison system is being privatized, the private and public sectors

cooperate in the health care and social assistance sectors, the "dangerously insane" can be put in private as well as public institutions, et cetera.

Alongside the more traditional "exclusionary mode of social control," with its disciplinary incarcerations, isolation, and stigmatization, Cohen (1985) also sees the development of an "inclusionary mode of social control," which aims to promote reintegration, inclusion, and control within society. The merging of the two control systems has far-reaching consequences. If the disciplinary part remains untouched, it offers the justification for the creation within the controlling option of a slew of new interventions at a lower level, including forensic social care, ambulant assistance, but also the core family, the neighborhood. Since these interventions target (re)integration and have to employ nonprofessional and institutional controllers, everybody is ultimately given a controlling function. The framework of social control becomes omnipresent yet fuzzy. Finally, the system of voluntary control can only be effective if there are enough emergency measures leading to tougher interventions; the continuum provides for a tough backup approach which always lurks in the background. "On the soft side there is indefinite inclusion, on the hard side, rigid exclusion" (Cohen 1985). Cohen (1979) calls it "the punitive city."

It appears that a new series of social science disciplines and categories is becoming entrenched in the control framework. This process develops alongside the way in which the more classic social sciences interact with the disciplines. Science takes ever new twists and turns or just emerges (e.g., leisure sciences and leisure management). The emergence of the different control and manipulation techniques spawns numerous disciplines which soon earn the status of science: administration sciences, marketing, and management ride the latest wave. The wielding of power has turned into a science.

It comes as no surprise that information technology and the development of the many subsidiary products are an important impetus in the continued development of the "controlling society." Countless digital applications can increase control over individual behavior. Information technology not only increases the effectiveness of static disciplinary mechanisms and institutions, it also, and primarily, has a fundamental role in the creation of the comprehensive and reinforced control system. The permanent creation of public and private databases and the possibilities of the media, telematics, and the information superhighway become technical extensions and improve the accuracy of the disciplinary framework. Through the creation of accurate data-gathering techniques, information technology generates new means to reinforce panopticism, the disciplinary tactics, the automatic surveillance and the permanent visibility. Surveillance, a cornerstone of power relationships since the dawn of capitalism, becomes more efficient (see Anthony Giddens in a *Contemporary Critique of Historical Materialism*). Human elements in the long chain of control, command, and notification can be replaced by and supplemented with cameras, microphones, badges, magnetic strips, chips, and so forth.

The American sociologist Gary Marx unmistakably points out the central role of technology in the "maximum security society." It can program life up to a point by technically excluding certain behavioral alternatives: automatic speed limits in cars, blocking external calls in companies, incorporated alcohol tests in cars, ID security tests based on voice or fingerprints, search term limits on the Internet. The computer also promotes the use of statistic projection in the decision-making process, increasing the use of elaborate profiles. Real individuals are managed to meet the standards of virtual simulations and ideal statistical profiles. Another characteristic of the "maximum security society" is the fact that everybody cooperates in the process of automatic (self-)surveillance. It needs to be pointed out that such a controlling society is marked by exposure and pervasive suspicion.

It is easy to come up with an electronic control mechanism which at any given moment can provide the position of one or all elements in an open environment. That way it can manage both the individual and overall movement, depending on the set (and changeable) objectives and intervening conditions. One example is an expert system which organizes a subway or rail network and which, in case of an accident or breakdown, can immediately come up with a safe and time-efficient solution for each train. Such an overall control system seems to be just as feasible for animals in a nature park, employees in a company, detainees within a limited space—electronic leashes for some, electronic cards for others, and perhaps electronic chips for all in the future.

From a technical viewpoint, it is not that far-fetched to extend this vision to the whole social area. The proliferation of automatic processing and the possible interlinkage already allow for relatively precise spotting and control. Digital personal data or such data which can be swiftly digitalized are already omnipresent, as mentioned in chapter 1. They threaten to expose every action of individuals, without the slightest need for closed institutions. They also allow the creation of global statistical overviews of consumer patterns, activities, travel, health, labor, et cetera. On top of that, data can be commercialized. Universities, for example, sell lists of their graduates to salesmen eager to set up target publicity lists, car companies sell their client database, credit reference systems are popular since they publicize lists of people with difficulties paying off their debt, and so on, ad infinitum. There have already been references to a whole series of technical devices which allow individuals to supervise one another: wiretapping equipment, video, supersensitive microphones, security systems, and electronic leashes which start beeping once a dog, a child, or another person leaves a preset area. The success of these devices only illustrates the pervasive suspicion of the "maximum security society."

The disciplinary system was characterized by preset normalizing mechanisms and remained linked to time and space. Instead, the innovating control framework seeks to have an immediate reaction to events. It is control in real time. Successive multistage development processes are replaced by instant interventions and modulations. The "itinerary" can be reassessed based on the efficiency with which the goal, another potential changing factor, is pursued. Information technology promotes the permanent reorganization and flexibility of controls.

We have not referred to privacy as such over the last few pages. The developments under discussion, however, run counter to the interests of privacy in a democratic constitutional state—the freedom to be oneself, to take independent decisions, and not to jump on the majority's bandwagon. Privacy means to be unaffected by permanent influence and manipulation. Well, the controlling societies and the surveillance framework are the absolute opposite. Against such a background, it is obvious that the privacy chants are increasingly out of sync.

But let's take this one step further. Mass communication, based on much the same technology, is reinforcing this controlling framework. Radio and television, newspapers, magazines, movies, and Websites are an important part of spiritual life. The emancipatory potential, however, clashes with this vision. Any which way one looks at this, it is numbing, dull fare, which the mass media and marketing companies sell around the globe. In this sense, mass media have become de facto active collaborators in the promotion of conformity. Even if their effect is indirect and convoluted, it is beyond doubt that, by amusing and numbing the mind, the mass media have the same effect as intensive surveillance or terror—cripple resistance. The contemporary fascination with the virtual universe is an added boon for the forces of normalization. Freedom and resistance slip a little further off the road.

Privacy's freedom is facing ever-broader, ever-stronger opposition. Normalization, disciplinary action, controls, surveillance and a general sense of numbing all clash with the ideals of the democratic constitutional state. The loud, unanimous chants backing the concept of privacy are quickly dying down. But perhaps it should also be said that the increase in the freedom of movement and thought during the twentieth century was only possible because of the sophistication of the overall social control mechanisms. In that case, the legal claim for individual privacy and freedom is more a symbolic story that makes the exercise of power bearable instead of a liberating practice and a show of opposition. The history of private life offers a paradox in which the argumentative cult of privacy ambiguously merges with an increasing and differentiated encroachment upon private space. If this is the case, we should all join the privacy chorus. Singing probably relieves the mind and may even provide the illusion of a good conscience for those who profit from invasions of privacy as well as for those who have resigned themselves to normalization and forced exposure.

Even though it is becoming increasingly difficult, there is the need to go down another road. Even a mere shred of confidence in the democratic constitutional state—if only for lack of a convincing alternative—forces an individual to take privacy's freedom seriously, because if this concept of privacy is excessively eroded, totalitarianism is closing in. The lack of shame and fear of those who profit from the development of the control and surveillance societies has to be met head-on by just as much shamelessness and fearlessness of those who resist them in the public sphere. They have to claim the most essential freedoms and rights that society provides. Each invasion of privacy needs to be justified and, sometimes, it will be acceptable. Sometimes, it will not be. It is the way the system works. What is certainly not acceptable is the veiled, creeping erosion of freedom, especially when it is accompanied by a hypocritical glorification of privacy.

Much is at stake. Citizens, judges, and legislators alike must assume their responsibility. Citizens can offer resistance, in practical terms and through the law. They have to insist on balancing their privacy freedom with the other interests at stake. It is extremely important to be radical since the values at stake are essential. Judges have to take privacy for what it is: a pillar of the legal system. It deserves to have its own weight within the balancing of interests. An additional argument to safeguard privacy is the fact that its erosion is progressing quickly. It should serve warning to legislators when they set social rules. Legislators should also take care to limit the number of legal invasions of privacy and make sure it becomes easier for civilians to resist such invasions.

The final section investigates how this was dealt with in "data protection law." Do the current developments counter the controlling societies by highlighting emancipatory privacy? Or are they just an empty shell appeasing resistance and soothing consciences?

Neotribalism, Nationalism, and Collective Identities

The end of the Cold War, the collapse of communism, the gradual disintegration of the welfare state, the drastic increase of economic insecurity, and the loss of optimism have doubtless all been a fertile soil for neotribalism to take root. This tribalism is no longer reduced to so-called underdeveloped people, but now it also is a major success story in the West and the former Eastern bloc countries. Countless nations, groups, and clans claim a collective identity based on ethnic, religious, cultural, moral, historic, economic, or other grounds. Their political programs, though, may vary widely. Sometimes, they claim "collective rights." But mostly, they aim for political fragmentation and the split-up of multicultural sovereign states in new unicultural or uninational, and thus tribal, states. There are examples galore. Just think of the forces at work in the former Yugoslavia, the former Soviet Union, and ex-Czechoslovakia; and the Basque, Breton, "Padanian," Quebecois, Walloon, and Flemish nationalists. Think of the independence movements in Tibet, Myanmar, Sri Lanka, Irian Jaya, Nigeria, and so on. Think of the Rwanda and Burundi killing fields, the Kurdish liberation movement, the Palestinian issue, and the claims of North and South American Indians, the aboriginals in Australia, the Maori in New Zealand, and the countless indigenous peoples in Asia, all with their own tribal claims.

In all those cases, the groups rely on the existence of a unifying "us" to lay a claim to the maintenance and expansion of the perceived collective identity. Sometimes this claim is a show of resistance, reacting to discrimination of the group as group (e.g., the Kurds, Palestinians, Karen), sometimes it is group-centered egoism (e.g., Flanders, Padania). Of course, the demands to create new homogenous tribal states and the subsequent disintegration of sovereign nations have caused very delicate problems at the level of international law. The right to self-determination of peoples, as it is upheld in international law since 1945, is effectively the right to decolonization. It justifies the resistance against foreign domination, yet without affecting territorial integrity.

But this is beside the point here. The theme is addressed because all claims to enshrine a collective identity and collective rights clash with the freedom of individual self-determination, and, as a result, privacy. To put it bluntly: this is true by definition no matter how good or bad the cause may seem.

Nationalist claims run counter to privacy's freedom because they radically deny interindividual social diversity. The insistence on a group identity implies that the differences between individuals are reduced to differences between groups. Generic names become more important than proper names and membership of a group is deemed to determine individual personality. This does not only apply to nationalism, but to other group claims as well. Feminism has gender as a decisive criterion; the gay movement has sexual disposition. Marxism thrives on class (the social position determines individual consciousness), et cetera. This point is made not to deny individuals the right to identify with one or other group. To the contrary, this is part of privacy's freedom. But it makes the demand to base rights and duties on socalled real affiliation to a group, no less problematic.

There simply are no criteria to determine, to a lesser or greater extent, a people or group. Neither blood, race, territory, biology, language, national character (*Volksgeist*), religion, nor culture can sufficiently or reasonably differentiate, because these aspects (sidestepping the relevance of the exercise) are never "pure." The characteristics are always mixed and intertwined, historically determined and in motion. They are linked with each other in a most individual way.[4] Nevertheless, nationalist and other collective identity claims single-mindedly continue to rely on the almost idiotic glorification of a few fossilized traits of individuals. These individuals are then reduced to one or a few of their many personality components. They become only man or woman, black or white, gay or straight, Croat or Serb, Hutu or Tutsi, punk or disco, and so forth. This way, it is assumed that everything, yes, everything, has been said about their action, thought, character, conviction, rights, duties, and so forth. This is very bad news for privacy's freedom which protects the myriad individual differences and projects of personal freedom. Individuals are not a simple, lasting, and static amalgam of two or three components. Instead they are, in the words of the French philosopher Michel Serres, a *métissage*. They continuously change when they interact with others, with ideas, with things and experiences. They are inextricably linked with the contexts of their lives. It makes the reliance on one element, one all-encompassing identity, irreconcilable with each individual life. How dull would life be if one's identity would develop naught throughout life? What would the point of privacy's freedom be? Instead, identity is the result of individual self-determination, which itself is in permanent motion. It also is defined by the autonomy to engage in relations or to be influenced by the development of groups. Each and every individual is unique and different, and it is exactly from this point of view that all individuals are equal. They have to respect each other as equals in their diversity and individual difference. As we discussed before, this is exactly what privacy is about.

The fact that the collective claims clash with the essential value of privacy is an indication of how deep-rooted the problem is. This is so because nationalist claims are both exclusive and inclusive. First, to the outside world, the group claim is per definition *exclusive*. The definition of a collective identity always entails that boundaries are set, excluding others for one reason or another. From the horrors of ethnic cleansing to the petty linguistic squabbling in Belgium and Canada, one group considers itself better than the next. There is the proud "us" with no equal in sight, only inferior, guilty, dangerous, different, and suspect others. Second, nationalist claims are also problematic looking within. They are *inclusive*. To embed the collective claim in reality, internal, individual differences have to be ignored. The collective identity calls for uniformity and discipline. It forces complex individual identities into restraining, one-dimensional models which are usually based on the visions of the leaders within a group. Everybody can be chained to one group through blood feud, terror, and fear (Hutus and Tutsis; Serbs Croats and Bosnian Muslims; Kosovar Serbs and ethnic Albanians). It can also be established through identity-inducing legislation and policy (Belgium's "language communities"). It again threatens the right to self-determination of individuals.

What's more, nationalist claims and collective rights cannot be reconciled with human rights, because the latter are based on humanism (an individual has them because he is human), universalism (they apply, whatever the situation, race, nationality, et cetera), and rationalism (they are a product of the Enlightenment and rational thought). Compared, collective rights lean heavily on collectivism (group interests are more important than individual freedom), particularism (human rights are no longer universal but granted to certain groups), and mysticism (irrational and holy attachment to nation, religion, the people, and race sweeps rationalism aside). The tension between both concepts is harrowing. If the law also considers that an individual is predetermined by his or her attachment to a group or people, what is left of the individual freedom to self-determination and privacy, both of which are a cornerstone of human rights?

Finally, and this will come as no surprise, the countless nationalist claims also clash with the core principles of the democratic constitutional states, which are amply described in chapter 2. In such states, the individual is the key actor. Individuals are protected against power, even against the majority. A majority does not have unlimited rights. It is restricted in its actions. This makes the democratic constitutional state per definition pluralist and diversified. The minority is no slave to the majority and individuals have fundamental rights and freedoms. We can echo Alain Touraine (1994) in saying that a national society which is culturally homogeneous is per definition antidemocratic: *Quod erat demonstrandum*. The unambiguous consequence of this is that a democratic constitutional state should never be allowed to impose one identity—be it religious, ethnic, cultural, linguistic or scientific. To the contrary, it must allow for the development of countless identities, going against all totalitarian claims. This is exactly privacy's role. Diversity is protected. Never will one message be allowed to dominate the whole discourse. Nationalism has a radically opposed program.

But on the other hand, personal freedom also implies that everyone is free to believe that he or she is predetermined by language, territory, national character, religion, blood, or whatever; act this way, be proud of it, and use it as a political platform. It is the very reason for the existence of freedom of speech, freedom of association, freedom of conscience, and privacy's freedom. These fundamental freedoms are obviously first individual prerogatives. But they also set out legal and political beacons for common political action and group bonding which can be used to boost a collective identity. This, however, can only be accepted if they respect the rights and freedoms of others, the public interest, and the common project which make such discourse possible. Collective action should not make a mockery of everyone's right not to join the collective groundswell. No one should suffer discrimination because of it. Everybody is free to choose whether to become part of a group or a network and whether to leave it or not. Nobody should be forced into anything, whatever the reason. Privacy is the freedom to be oneself.

Free individuals are and remain the cornerstone of democratic constitutional society. Their freedom of choice remains preeminent and takes precedence over collective cultural, religious, or ethnic identity claims, which implies the latter should not become a normative standard. It does not stop groups and collective entities, however, to act as subjects and actors. To the contrary, they are essential in the relationship between power and resistance. It only means that those groups or collective entities—which are in fact networks in motion—must always be able to be deconstructed as networks of individuals who freely join in a common pursuit. Otherwise, there is no freedom left and the democratic constitutional state has failed.

Notes

1. J. Weizenbaum, *Computerkracht en mensenmacht: Van oordeel tot berekening* (Amsterdam: Contact, 1984), 42 (our translation).

2. Cf. *"Aucun savoir ne se forme sans un système de communication, d'enregistrement, d'accumulation, de déplacement qui est en lui-même une sorte de forme de pouvoir et qui est lié dans son existence et son fonctionnement aux autres formes de pouvoir. Aucun pouvoir, en revanche, ne s'exerce sans l'extraction, l'appropriation, la distribution ou la retenue d'un savoir. A ce niveau il n'y a pas la connaissance d'un côté, et la société de l'autre, ou la science et l'Etat mais les formes fondamentales du 'pouvoir-savoir.' "* M. Foucault, *Résumé des cours: 1970–1982* (Paris: Julliard, Conférences, essais et leçons du Collège de France, 1989), 20.

3. *"Sans doute l'objectif principal aujourd'hui n'est-il pas de découvrir, mais de refuser ce que nous sommes."* M. Foucault, "Deux essais sur le sujet et le pouvoir," in *Michel Foucault: Un parcours philosophique,* edited by H. Dreyfus and P. Rabinow (Paris: Gallimard, 1984), 308.

4. Let's take "pure blood" as a criterion, and then it suffices to go back only a few generations to find ancestors with different blood: everybody has "mixed blood." Let's take race or biological characteristics as criteria, and biologists and genetic scientists will immediately sweep these arguments off the table. They have known for a long time that apart from homozygote twins, no two human beings have an identical genetic pattern. As such, they showed that race concept, as well as race discrimination, is not based on any scientific evidence. Culture (be it language, religion, morals, et cetera) as a distinctive criterion is also rife with problems. Culture as a whole is mixed, an amalgam, subject to countless quirks of history, as are culture's components. Cultures are alive and interactive, and fortunately they are never a finished product. They are in development and evolve through internal movement and contacts with outside influences. They never are "once and for all." They never are an essence.

CHAPTER FIVE

Privacy and the Processing of Personal Data

Determining Standards

Privacy is a crucial issue in our Western society. It is the result of the intertwining of elementary and daily aspects of life with the different concepts of privacy, such as determining one's personality without outside interference; making autonomous decisions on spiritual, physical, intimate, social, and family issues without interference; carving one's way through life without outside pressure; and so on. Let's not repeat it all again—privacy covers the freedom to be oneself. Yet privacy is not universal, not eternal. Some cultures and religions have a strong community imprint and consider it only natural to intervene in private life. The historical, cultural, and legal comparative perspective provides plenty of examples. Privacy is closely aligned with individual independence, interindividual differences, and the pluralism of choices in life which are the cornerstones of Western democratic constitutional states. In short, privacy is an essential part of our societies.

Because privacy is intimately interwoven with individual freedom, it is undefined, contextual, relational, and nonabsolute. It is undefined because freedom implies a multitude of choices and possibilities. It is contextual because the lack of clear privacy criteria means that each case has to be judged by itself, based on all relevant aspects. It is relational because the issue of privacy always implies at least two actors. It is nonabsolute because the freedom of one individual inevitably comes face-to-face with the freedoms of all others, including the public interest. Hence, protecting privacy means that an interest with fluctuating and "soft" characteristics has to be made "hard." Understandably, this is a complex and delicate affair, and the outcome always depends on different actors, facts, and decisions.

In practice this is not easy. Entrenching privacy in a capitalist society thriving on free-market economics is problematic, even paradoxical. This economy produces imbalances in power, insists on exposure, and does not grant everyone the same possibilities. Despite its intentions to undo economic wrongs, the welfare state pries deep into the individual lives of its citizens, seeking to organize and manage society. If we take the aforementioned dangers into account (technical possibilities, normalization, control and neotribalism), the diagnosis is depressing. Some analysts have been quick to jump to the conclusion that privacy has been effectively eroded.

We will not go down that road. Attacks on and threats against the freedom of privacy, whatever their origin, always have to do with power relations and their inherent tension. The strategic positions of the actors will steer the choices, decisions, and behavior of one actor in particular. During that process, resistance and freedom are curtailed. Privacy is emancipatory because it becomes the guardian of the weak party in the power relationship. When alternative behavior, free choice, and autonomy are under threat, privacy has to be taken seriously by the legal system and considered as such by the courts. It does not mean that the privacy claim necessarily needs to be accepted. No, it is important that, at some stage, the different interests can be considered. It is law's primary task to prevent, through mediation, power relations from becoming absolute: privacy is a concept which allows law to fulfill that task. But the mere "balancing act" is insufficient. Instead, the constitutional weight that privacy carries has to be taken seriously into account. Moreover, this weight should be even further increased because various social developments have put privacy under more and more pressure. Nowadays, the emancipatory use of privacy should go beyond the fact that legislators, judges, and administrators give it sufficient consideration. They also have to run a permanent catch-up operation to make sure that privacy can play its full role as counterweight in the face of new, threatening developments. Privacy's score sheet is pretty negative so far. All the more reason to protect personal freedom.

The gathering, storage, processing, and use of personal data are—it has been said before—an integral part of interhuman relations. They apply to the economic as well as to micro- and macropolitical balances of power. The disciplinary apparatus, control, normalization, and surveillance would be nothing without information gathering. The same applies to countless social activities which are affected by power relations: labor, education, trade, consumption, administration, travel, et cetera. The optimal gathering of information on individuals contributes greatly to the much-desired increase in efficiency or productivity.

Techno-scientific developments, especially the seemingly endless proliferation of information technology applications, contribute to a palpable performance increase of data gathering and processing. Techno-scientific developments not only improve the effectiveness of these activities but also increase the threat that privacy will lose out. They highlight power relations which are already problematic. Electronic applications greatly increase the number of processing, linkage, and selection possibilities. Today, an individual can easily be checked on and rendered fully transparent. Automation allows for permanent surveillance. Any behavior will be easier to check because it leaves more and more electronic traces. The result is that freedom suffers: individuals adapt themselves much easier if they know their actions can be checked or retraced. The production of induced behavior and the functioning of the power structure become more effective because of the increased possibilities of real-time and a posteriori control. Information technology in principle consolidates power.[1] It promotes and refines the methods of control, exposure, surveillance, normalization, and manipulation. Add the fact that the power of those who use information technology is often already bigger to start with. The stream of personal data primarily flows from the weak actors to the strong. Citizens not only need to provide information to the authorities, but they also need to do so as tenant, job seeker, customer, loan applicant, and patient.

We can now set out, in theory, what the general standards are that special legislation on personal data processing should meet to effectively contribute to the emancipatory challenge of privacy. As of now, they can be used as references and guidelines during the discussions on the main points of the Directive 95/46/EC of the European Parliament and of the Council (see the appendix) of 24 October 1995 on the protection of individuals with regard to the processing of personal data and on the free movement of such data (or the EC Directive).

In the first place, special rules need to consider the fact that personal data processing, in principle, violates privacy's freedom. This implies that a general ban on processing should be the core principle. At the same time, though, data processing will be legitimate if based on a consideration of the interests at stake. The interests of processing must be weighed against the invasion of privacy it causes. The approach is in line with Article 8 of the

European Convention on Human Rights (ECHR): the processing of personal data is in principle illegal, but exemptions can be obtained if certain conditions are met.

Second, special legislation needs to offer a stronger and more accurate protection of privacy than the provisions of international human rights law and constitutional values have provided so far. Article 8 of the ECHR certainly does apply to the manual and automatic processing of personal information. Any processing can only be legitimate if it meets the terms of Article 8 of the ECHR. In this context, the existing protection needs to be increased. In any other case, the operation would be useless and misleading.

Third, privacy's freedom has to carry a lot of weight in the scales of Justice, fully in line with the fundamental role and hierarchal position of privacy within society. But it also needs to redress an already unacceptable situation which has steadily worsened. With the massive processing of personal data, public and private actors have put society before a fait accompli. The legal protection component needs to be improved to meet the challenges of the practice of power which has already spilled beyond its borders. Privacy is in danger and the automation of personal data processing only worsens the situation. The new rules primarily need to come to the aid of privacy. The balance of power needs to be pushed this way.

Fourth, since privacy's freedom is constantly at risk, any special legislation must make sure that the legitimacy of every single piece of processing can be legally challenged by each data subject. For each separate data processing case, law needs to be able to fulfill its role as mediator. This is why generalizations are incompatible with the nature of privacy's freedom. Privacy depends on context and on the specific relations between the different factors in each case—the respective interests of the people involved, their social role and impact on power, the aim of the disputed data processing, the application of the data concerned, and so forth.

Fifth and finally, a specific law should take the existing imbalances in power relations into account. Privacy's freedom and the resistance of the individuals concerned need to be reinforced to make them stronger when they face their powerful opponents. When it comes to data processing, the imbalance in power is often poignant. Information processors usually have more power than their data subjects and influence their behavior. This process has to be anticipated, for example, by providing a whole range of effective ways to resist interference, keep the procedural threshold low, create a powerful entity which can, on its own initiative, defend the interests of the data subject's privacy, et cetera.

Data Protection: The More Privacy, the Less Privacy?

The interest that national and international institutions take in personal data processing is not new. A series of initiatives goes back to the early 1970s. Germany (1977) and France (1978) were the first European states to agree on specific legislation. Most other European states followed suit over the next two decades (the United Kingdom in 1984, the Netherlands in 1990, and Belgium in 1993). International organizations encouraged, even forced, them to adopt such measures. The guidelines of the Organization of Economic Cooperation and Development (OECD) governing the protection of privacy and transborder flows of personal data of 23 September 1980 are such a case. The Council of Europe's Convention 108 of 28 January 1981 for the protection of individuals with regard to automatic processing of personal data is another. The latest and most stringent initiative in the list is the aforementioned EC Directive, which was worked out in the framework of the European Union.

The broad lines of these legal texts run in parallel and together they begat "data protection law." Time and again, the legal texts refer to the same core principles of personal data protection or the "data protection principles." They are primarily prevalent in the OECD Guidelines and Convention 108, but the essence was already part of the 6 January 1978 French law *relative a l'informatique, aux fichiers et aux libertés*. All the elements come back in the EC Directive. In summary, the core principles stipulate that personal data may be collected fairly and lawfully. However, they can only be processed to achieve clearly specified, explicit, and legitimate objectives. Bans are imposed on the processing of certain kinds of information, for example, race, ethnic origin, political opinions, religious or philosophical beliefs, trade union membership, health, or sex life. Data subjects acquire specific rights. Controls such as the right of access to data about them and the right to correction are recognized in the texts. A special public supervisory entity has to be created to exert effective control over data processing and the quality of processed data.

It should come as no surprise that, from a sociological point of view, the core principles in the various initiatives are broadly similar. After all, they were the result of fruitful cooperating between working and expert groups under the auspices of the OECD, the Council of Europe, and the European Commission. The similarity is also understandable from another perspective. Economic and administrative interests benefit from harmonized rules since they facilitate the cross-border transfer of personal data. We discuss this in more detail later.

Yet it is remarkable that the data protection principles are the result of very divergent institutions. In the considerations accompanying the texts, they all stress different sensitivities. It is the reason why it is relevant to focus on the origin, motivation, and goals of the three aforementioned international initiatives since they so clearly put their stamp on national legal systems.

The OECD Guidelines were endorsed by the member states, yet they are nonbinding. However, they do express a morally binding consensus on data protection principles and they are supposed to offer a general framework on which to base national legislation. The guidelines subscribe to the core principles of the protection of personal data.[2] They include private and public, computerized, and manual processing of personal data.

An obvious question is why an organization which centers on economic growth of the world's wealthiest states is suddenly concerned about the privacy of individuals. Yet paradoxical as it may seem, it is easy to understand. Much more than seeking to protect privacy, the OECD is trying to create an international legal area within which personal data can freely circulate. Government intervention and protectionism in international data transactions must be curtailed. The OECD wants to erase any difference between legislation in member states since divergence in the protection of privacy could be used by OECD states to regulate and limit such data traffic. A state which offers a high privacy protection threshold can ban the export of data to a nation with a low threshold. This is why the OECD Guidelines want to create equivalent protection. The OECD's point of departure is that the joint acceptance of the data protection principles will erase any reason for government intervention. It also implies that the privacy bar should not be put too high in the member states. Otherwise, it will again be the cause of imbalance and possibly obstruct the free flow of personal data.

Personal data are an asset. The motive driving the whole debate is the free flow of information, not privacy. The OECD's main concern is economic and this is fully in line with the purpose of the organization. So it is only natural that the OECD Guidelines serve the interest of the economic forces, which need a profitable fast and free international flow of data. Such flows, for example, for the banking and insurance sector, are obviously important because they are performing instruments of market control, administration, and organization. The assessment of individual cases and global situations offers new insights. Furthermore, the increased mobility of personal data increases their value and reach as a market asset. In short, the important economic powers take center stage, not the individual citizen. So from the start, the standards are skewed. The minimum rules on privacy are in fact used to attain a different, and ironically even an opposite, goal: smoothing the free flow of personal data.

However, the OECD presents its guidelines as a result of a careful balancing act involving both the interests of privacy and the free flow of information, which it considers hierarchal equals. This is misleading because the question can be rightly asked, What exactly dpes the free flow of privacy-sensitive data have to do with the freedom of information, speech, and communication? In reality, these flows primarily serve economic, organizational, and administrative interests. And this should push the legal balance privacy's way. However, this is not what has happened. It even gets worse when it turns out that the result of the balance of interests has already been predetermined in favor of the free flow of personal data. Per definition, this increases the dangers that privacy faces. What privacy gains on the one hand (minimum standards of protection), it loses on the other (free flow). This is the only way forward for the OECD. From the start, it excludes the option that more controls on data flows improve the protection of privacy. It raises the question of whether the OECD Guidelines are little more than a privacy-friendly front hiding the true purpose of promoting an economic policy which puts personal data on the same level as any other economic product. The establishment of a minimum level of legal protection of personal data to compensate for their effective international traffic is a disappointing result. It is all the more so because personal data has abundantly moved across borders since 1980 while national legislations still have to prove they will be more than just empty talk.

The Council of Europe is a more obvious international institution to tackle the issue of privacy and personal data processing. The main aim of the organization is the promotion of human rights in its member states. convention 108 is binding and obliges the member states to take the necessary legislative measures to make the principles stick at a national level. The Convention can only be ratified afterwards. Because of this, Convention 108 has had a major impact on many European national legislations, including Belgium and the Netherlands.

Convention 108 obliges the member states to implement a series of basic principles of data protection.[3] They roughly resemble the principles of the OECD Guidelines. The treaty applies to automatically processed personal data in both the private and public sectors. If need be, it can be extended to include manually processed data and information on legal persons.[4] But here, too, the national implementation of the "basic principles for data protection" has to meet the need for transborder data flow, unhindered by roadblocks, bans, or licensing systems. Equivalent protection among ratifying states again has to create a fundamental ban on the control of data traffic.

It is logical that the Council of Europe puts more emphasis on the protection of private life in comparison with the substantially similar initiative of the OECD. Convention 108 is explicitly in line with Articles 8 and 10 of the ECHR. It refers to the balancing of interests between privacy, freedom of information, and freedom of speech, a common practice in the ECHR framework. Yet here again, privacy needs to be reconciled with the unlimited transborder flow of personal data. The treaty preamble's last consideration recognizes that "it is necessary to reconcile the fundamental values of the respect for privacy and the free flow of information between peoples." Without much consideration, the point of departure is that "the transfer across national borders, by whatever medium, of personal data undergoing automatic processing or collected with a view to their being automatically processed" is the reflection of the freedom of information in a computerized environment. The relation between the electronic flows of personal data and the freedom of speech is far from evident. The question can be rightly asked, with François Rigaux's irony, exactly what the relation is between the electronic data flow, with its very specific recipients and senders and the "free flow of information between peoples." In any case, it is easier to prove that these data flows serve economic interests or other control and management strategies. Seen from this perspective, there is an increasing suspicion that the freedom of information and speech is purely used to counter privacy.

Again, the issue is ambiguous. The treaty parties must have a minimal equivalent and legal privacy protection framework in place to clinch the free flow of transborder personal data traffic. So the implementation of the rules to protect privacy goes hand in hand with the confirmation of the practice which threatens it. What's more, the states commit themselves not to check and restrict the export of personal data to other signatory states. Instead of protectionism, we get deregulation. The free flow of personal information within international networks is given an official government escort. Convention 108 also leads to the isolation of countries without privacy rules, or "data havens." So these countries too are forced to adopt privacy legislation.

Much like the OECD Guidelines, Convention 108 also is a coin with two distinct sides. Even if it contributes to the establishment of national privacy rules on personal data processing, it does not meet privacy's concerns. Privacy has not had a sufficient impact on the treaty, which has failed to galvanize privacy's catch-up operation: The processing of personal data is probably taken care of but also immediately justified. In fact, data flows which escape control are not limited but legitimized.

The European Commission claimed that the OECD Guidelines and Convention 108 did not produce the desired result, and in 1990, it started laying the groundwork for a directive on the processing of personal data. It took all of five years, though, and an immense amount of lobbying and politicking in the European Parliament before the directive became a fact. Even though most of the European Union member states are already parties to Convention 108, the Commission considered the differences between the national legislations too important. It considered this a serious obstacle in the completion of the internal market since it could impede the transborder flows of personal data. At the time, some member states were already well on their way to becoming data havens (Belgium), while the legislative process in others had stalled. The Commission deemed that all this had a negative impact on the core principles of the EU: the free market; the free traffic of goods, people, services, and capital; free enterprise; and a series of economic activities at EU level. The Commission also insisted on the development of the European information technology industry and the internal market of telecommunication equipment and services. They all needed harmonized rules on privacy protection and personal data processing.

The European Midas is at work again: everything the Commission touches becomes a market. A lot of EU texts may often highlight the fundamental importance of the rights and freedoms of its citizens; the lowdown of any initiative, however, can often be reduced to the necessity to achieve the single internal market. Competition distortions caused by divergences among member states have to be eradicated. Market laws are elevated to the level of laws of nature and are considered untouchable. Safeguarding the interest of privacy is not a goal in itself. The concern about privacy is totally subordinate to the market prerogatives. Jacques Fauvet, the former director of *Le Monde* and former chairman of France's *Commission Nationale Informatique et Liberté*, put it this way: In the EC initiative, data protection is more a condition for economic development than an answer to counter the threats to individual freedom by performing technology. This conclusion is not unexpected. The goals of the European institutions are primarily economic and, in the end, this also determines the authority of the European Commission.

Despite all this, the Commission does put the privacy protection bar high. This can be read word for word in the tenth consideration of the EC Directive and it was a goal from the start. The Commission emphatically links its choice to the importance that the European institutions attach to democracy and the fundamental rights of citizens. The tenth consideration specifically refers to Article 8 of the ECHR and to the fact that privacy is recognized in the general principles of community law. A weakening of the existing level of protection should be avoided at all cost. In the same vein, the directive proclaims that it will "give substance to and amplify" the principles of Convention 108. The establishment of a high level of protection must nevertheless be seen in light of the political impossibility of setting a harmonized low threshold. The main aim of this effort is to erase barriers limiting the free flow of personal data traffic through the establishment of an equivalent level of privacy protection. Of course, this cannot imply that some member states should reduce their established level of protection. The reduction of privacy protection to the lowest common denominator not only would make a mockery of the national efforts to protect privacy but also of Convention 108. The European legislator has thus been forced to impose a high level of privacy protection because it had to take existing laws and international legal instruments into account. From the start, industrial and financial lobbies attacked the initiative, calling it a patchwork of all of the most stringent elements from the different national legislations. It still remains to be seen whether the protection threshold level will really turn out to be this high in practice.

Much like the OECD Guidelines and Convention 108, the EC Directive is ambivalent. All three have in common that they legitimize the global effect of practices which invade privacy—both at the level of processing and international flows of personal data—through the creation of rules which purport to have a high level of privacy protection. The European Union pushes the legislative acrobatics to an extreme. It somehow achieves to link the legitimacy of the processing and the international flows of personal data with a "high" level of data protection.

An assessment of the overall design and true motives of the three international initiatives clearly illustrates the negative impact on privacy's freedom. The same applies to national legislations which have been approved in their wake. The aforementioned criteria are not met—first of all because the world has been turned topsy-turvy. The processing of personal data is taken care of, but it is allowed in principle and not prohibited. An outright processing ban effectively applies only to special categories of sensitive information. What's more, the states involved are prohibited in any way from intervening in mutual transborder personal data traffic. It is clear that the free flow of personal data takes precedence over privacy's freedom.

The norm-hierarchal weight of privacy is thus being underestimated. Privacy's freedom is forced to face interests which have been artificially pumped up to its level. It doesn't matter that much for data processing in the public sector since, unless proven otherwise, it always has the public interest at heart. When it comes to data processing in the private sector, however, one can see that such purely economic or administrative interests such as competitiveness, efficiency, competition, and deregulation are suddenly dressed up as information freedom and given the same norm-hierarchal importance. In most cases, though, it has nothing to do with this. Community law is less ambiguous since it simply rates economic freedom as high as privacy's freedom. As a result, privacy doesn't carry enough weight in a lopsided balance. The imbalance becomes all the more evident since the whole undertaking is aimed at a confirmation of the practical situation of processing and transmission of personal data and not at a positive reevaluation of privacy's freedom. For sure, certain excesses in personal data processing are curtailed, but there is no intention to push through genuine change. The computerization, the networks and information highways, and the potential to link and merge personal information are never questioned. The public debate and concerns about privacy have come too late.

Finally, the question can be asked, What exactly does data protection law have to do with the protection of the freedom of privacy of individuals? The motivations of the OECD Guidelines, Convention 108, and the EC Directive hardly touch upon the disproportionate balance of power between the data processors and subjects, the behavioral control and the means of control which emanate from data processing, the increased threats from international data flows, and so on. The essence of privacy's freedom is lacking. Beyond a doubt, the resistance and complaints about the lack of privacy are the root of the initiatives. The public demands for more privacy, echoed by some political forces, have proved to be strong enough to put the wheels of international legislation in motion. This does not necessarily imply that privacy's freedom becomes the real objective. It is closer to the truth that a privacy obstacle is being circumvented. The true agenda quickly takes over again once the privacy issue is taken care of. And that agenda invariably centers on organizational, economic, administrative, and competitive optimization of the activities in the public and private sector.

Against the background of such an analysis of the core motives and objectives of personal data protection law, one can only conclude that the concept of privacy has a hollow ring to it. And it is not as if a global assessment of the current national legislations on privacy and their applications can improve the tune any. Naturally, results differ from country to country. But wherever one looks, nowhere has the power of the processors been significantly dented to improve privacy's freedom. Practical reality is not impressed by the law and only halfheartedly adapts itself. In addition, governments and supervisory institutions often cannot (or will not) cope with the administrative burden that such new rules entail. Marxists appear to be right: the capitalist market does not want to play second fiddle to human rights. Privacy is not a goal in itself but a means to achieve other goals. Even if the free market can live with some concessions, it will not yield an inch when it comes to the core issues. Freedom of trade and industry, competition, economic development, administrative efficiency, and techno-scientific progress take, de facto, precedence over personal freedom. Little wonder that the privacy dimensions of the three initiatives under review are called exaggerated and illusionary.

So is there no nuance left, and is our analysis too extreme? Is this a show of rabid skepticism and prejudice? Has privacy lost the good fight, or is there a glimmer of hope? Is there nothing positive to say about the three initiatives, especially the EC Directive? Or has privacy's freedom already been sacrificed on the altar of the free market? It is tough to answer these questions because the EC Directive and the preceding national and international rules are so ambiguous. It shows in the attitude they engender. One has to realize that the economic–technological logic takes precedence over human rights and that, at the same time, some concessions to promote privacy were made. Perhaps the best attitude is reflected in the saying, "One must make a virtue of necessity."

Anyway, the dice are cast. The EU member states have to apply the EC Directive. But the private and public players have preempted legislation and have applied information technology to massively process personal data. It has even become irrelevant to ask whether they worried about the implications on privacy. The facts speak for themselves. In a few seconds, personal data from around the world can merge into one whole. The globe is caught in a web of communication networks, to say nothing of satellite transmissions. Huge financial and economic interests are at stake. And so on.

Obviously, there is no way to turn back the hands of time. The legislators in the third millennium cannot sidestep the existing specific legal rules, technical means, economic interests and the power relations at every level. It is self-evident that the automation of data processing also has advantages for the individual. Privacy's freedom is not absolute and, at some point, has to make room for other interests. But this hardly erases the sobering approach of the skeptical deconstruction of personal data protection law. Personal freedom is still in danger and the initiatives that claim to defend it have a double edge. The defenders of privacy's freedom have no reason to cheer, because even their rhetoric has been hijacked.

There is thus a need for pragmatism and realism, even if it involves accepting the fait accompli, the artificially created needs, and the established balances of power. Idealism, fairness, and individual freedom are no match for the interests that have united to promote the legitimacy and deregulation of large-scale personal data processing. Resistance obviously has no other choice than to operate within the reality that is. It means that the ambiguous initiatives have to go beyond their original intentions to improve privacy protection. National legislators and judges have to nudge things in this direction and they should come to face their responsibility. To put it provocatively: the perverse initiatives have to be taken at their word. They need to be counterperverted as much as possible to effectively and truly boost privacy's freedom. The question is to what extent this is still possible.

As was mentioned earlier, the EC Directive aims to set a high level of protection. It would only be logical that the implementation of the directive opens doors to radicalize the interests of privacy in the new legislative initiatives. The next section assesses a series of aspects in the EC Directive from this perspective. There is a search for clues in the directive to improve the implementation of privacy's freedom as described beforehand. We do not go for an exhaustive or systematic analysis of the directive since that would reach beyond the purpose of this chapter. Instead, a series of exercises is discussed, according to the aforementioned five standards, on how to deal with the directive in a privacy-promoting way.

Making a Virtue of Necessity: Toward a Radical Privacy-Inspired Implementation of the EC Directive?

The EC Directive applies to the processing of personal data. This concept needs to cast its net as wide as possible and include automated and manual processing. The directive covers manual processing only if it constitutes a filing system and has a minimal structure, which does not apply to automated processing because computer programs have the capacity to merge and intertwine masses of loose data within seconds. The term "processing" also needs to be given a comprehensive interpretation. The directive imposes upon the member states a definition which says that it applies to any operation which is performed upon personal data. The rules cover each part of processing—

"collection, recording, organization, storage, adaptation or alteration, retrieval, consultation, use, disclosure by transmission, dissemination, or otherwise making available, alignment or combination, blocking, erasure, or destruction." Even the mere collection of personal data is covered by the directive. "Personal data" refers to "any information relating to an identified or identifiable natural person." There are no limits on content or technology. Phone numbers and license plates, social security numbers, images, voices, genetic information, and fingerprints are explicitly mentioned as personal data. A person is identifiable as soon as identification is possible based on means that can reasonably be assumed to be used by responsible processors.

All this is good news, because it means that video surveillance and other control systems will be subject to personal data processing legislation. Even better: image processors will have to apply the most stringent provisions of the directive, namely those dealing with the processing of special categories of sensitive data. This is because images contain information on racial or ethnic origin, health or religion of a person. The intention of the Commission to include images as personal data faced stiff resistance from lobbies defending the use of video surveillance. The counterargument of two authors in the banking sector, where video surveillance is rife, became memorable: they were worried about the fate of stamp collectors.

The directive says that personal data have to be processed fairly and lawfully. Processing will be lawful if it is done in accordance with the stipulations of the directive. Processing also has to be honest or "fair,"[5] a provision which is linked to the transparency principle and the desired openness of processing. The citizens involved have to be truly and fully informed about all phases and contexts of the processing procedure. Of course, this is a condition sine qua non for subsequent controls on data processing. It specifically applies to the gathering of personal data, which should not be based on secret, hidden, sly, or hypocritical methods. The secret, hidden gathering of information and the processing of data or the hidden use of microphones, cameras, listening devices, and detectors are thus banned. No openness, no legitimacy.[6]

The main principle of data protection law is the purpose specification principle. It also is at the heart of the EC Directive.[7] The processing of personal data is not banned, but allowed on the condition that the processing meets specified, explicit and legitimate purposes. Hence, the system's most important touchstone is the purpose or finality of processing. It provides the criteria to judge the legitimacy of processing and the quality of data and its use.

The idea that the separation of powers is a good way to keep those powers in check lies at the heart of the purpose specification principle. Because the power of the processors and the ability to influence behavior expands with their increase in exchanges, sales, linkages, groupings, analyses, and availability of personal data, their competence to process is limited to meet well-defined goals. In other words, processing operations are not banned but have to be separated.

The delineation of the processing purpose turns out to be the weak link in the protection system. Calls for the recognition of "catchall" purposes threaten to undermine the whole legislative framework. Such definitions of finalities as "make profit" or "contribute to whatever is of service to a person or corporation" do not impose any limits whatsoever. Any banker-insurer-tour operator-salesperson of personal data can do whatever he or she wants. On the other hand, the demand to have stringent specifications of purposes would become paralyzing and unworkable. It would create a massive amount of red tape. In ideal circumstances, the specific purpose of processing should be defined somewhere in between the two extremes, taking into account the constitutional weight of privacy's freedom and the necessity of a catch-up operation. One thing is clear, the criteria for delineation of one computerized processing operation cannot be found in the existence of something like a physical or technical set of operations. From the viewpoint of information technology, this is just unreal. Even the tiniest personal computer is able to process information with totally different finalities. Here, too, different processing operations must be separated.

The result of this is that the delineation and separation of purposes are decisive in the establishment of the number of processing operations. Finality is the key to pinpoint what the processing operation is. And since the whole protection system is engrafted onto the processing operation, it will succeed or fail based on the way in which processing is delineated. Personal data processing is each processing operation or series of operations with personal data which aims to realize one purpose, one finality. The processing delineation directly depends on the finality delineation. Thus: one purpose equals one processing operation.

All this doesn't mean, however, that one piece of personal data cannot be used by the same processor in several operations with different aims. But to make control on the use and quality of data effective, each processor needs to delineate the operations beforehand by describing precisely and explicitly what data will be processed to achieve what purpose. It will allow for an assessment of what data may or may not be combined. So there are two problems: the unlimited definitions of finality and the idea that a processing operation can have more than one finality. Because of this, there is the need for a radically negative attitude toward such concepts as "derived," "related," "implicit," and "secondary purposes." They threaten protection and should be excluded from legislation, even if Article 18 of the EC Directive mentions "several related purposes."

This, however, has not solved the touchy issue of the finality and processing delineation. The measure of precision in delineating the finality is proportional to the measure of privacy protection that it provides. Checking a processing operation which was not sufficiently delineated is de facto impossible. The answer to these problems can probably be found in a generic definition of the purpose. The data processor needs to differentiate between the different processing operations on a functional basis. In the end, it must be possible for a company or a public service to accurately identify and functionally delineate the different purposes of the organization. It will allow for the selection of what personal data can and cannot be used for in a processing operation to achieve one set purpose. With a bit of goodwill, vague and (illegal) all-encompassing definitions of finality should be easy to avoid. It suffices to have an insight into the different activities of an organization or company. "Wage management" processing consists of the sum of personal data operations necessary to pay salaries. There needs to be a strict separation, however, with the processing of "customer management," even if an individual is part of both categories. Not all information of both processing operations should be merged.

It is obviously not enough that the purpose of personal data processing should be clearly defined and well delineated. It also has to be justified and legitimate. This is stated explicitly in Article 7 of the EC Directive. Beyond a series of exceptions we will not address here,[8] legitimacy is based on three general principles. The first concerns processing operations to help fulfill government tasks and pursue the public interest by the authorities themselves or others working for them.[9] Government data processing has to meet the criteria of the judicial framework of the specific administrative authority and comply with its statutory powers. On top of that, each action by the authorities has to meet the criteria of the public interest. Mutatis mutandis, this also applies to the processing operations which the authorities manage or delegate. As a result, government data processing is not justified when it is not necessary for the exercise of a specific power of the administration concerned. It is just as unjustified when government data processing operations constitute a disproportionate invasion of privacy, since protection of privacy is to a large extent part of the public interest. There should be no less-invasive method available to achieve the same goal. On top of that, government data processing has to respect Article 8 of the ECHR. The restrictions set out in the second paragraph of that article fully apply. And apart from the aforementioned legitimacy and proportionality requirement, government data processing must be necessary in a democracy and also be "in the interest of national security, public safety, or the economic well-being of the country, for the prevention of disorder or crime, for the protection of health or morals or the protection of the rights and freedoms of others." Since personal data processing runs per definition counter to privacy, it implies that it will only be legitimate when it contributes to the realization of one or more of the goals set out in the second paragraph of Article 8. So a processing operation is not justified simply because it is executed by or for the government. National rules need to make this meticulously clear. They have to ensure and encourage that the judges and the specially created supervisory authorities consider the interests of every side in every situation.

A second legitimacy principle primarily concerns private processing of personal data. Article 7(f) of the EC Directive says that "processing is necessary for the purposes of the legitimate interests pursued by private interests, except where such interests are overridden by the interests for fundamental rights and freedoms of the data subject." Again, two aspects intertwine. First, the ultimate purpose of the processing should be lawful. An illegal or illegitimate interest can never be pursued by a legitimate processing operation. If the processing is undertaken by a legal person, its corporate purposes will be taken into account as an additional touchstone. Legal persons can only undertake action to achieve the goals laid out in their articles of association. The processing operation has to seamlessly fit in that concept. Second, the processing operation must be clearly necessary and indispensable to achieve the set purpose of the processor. Is it possible to achieve that purpose through other means? From privacy's viewpoint, is this the least harmful way? Proportionality and subsidiarity are essential. The interests have to be carefully balanced, taking into account their hierarchal entrenchment and the necessary catch-up operation to safeguard privacy's freedom. In each case, the concrete interests facing each other have to be carefully evaluated. A purely commercial purpose which necessitates a drastic invasion of privacy (e.g., the processing of personal data for direct marketing sales) has to be judged differently (and more severely) than data processing necessary to maintain public health, freedom of speech or, for that matter, the running of a sports club.

The third legitimacy principle is probably the most problematic. Article 7(a) states that "personal data may be processed only if the data subject has unambiguously given his consent." Consent means "any freely given specific and informed indication of his wishes by which the data subject signifies his agreement to personal data relating to him being processed" (Article 2[h], EC Directive). Processing of personal data is thus justified if the data subject clearly gives his or her consent after being informed of all aspects of the processing operation: the delineated and justified purpose of the processing operation, the categories of personal data which will be processed, possible third parties which will have access to the information, who is responsible, his or her rights, and so on. The unambiguity and specificity of the consent and the complete information on which it is based will need to be proved by the processor in case of conflict.

The consent criterion is doubtless in line with the concept of privacy as freedom. The individual is jointly responsible for the use and destination of information about him or her. Yet it also engenders difficulties. First of all, and as we have mentioned often before, the freedom of choice is in practice often a limited and relative one. Not everyone in our society has the same freedoms and possibilities. It may be an objective, but it is not a reality. Most personal data processing creates a relationship in which the data subject is the weak party in the balance of power. The behavior of a data subject is steered, the data flow is one-way. Most of the time, the data subject needs something (e.g., credit, health insurance) and is almost forced to give consent. The market forces require full exposure. In the end, consent is often turned into a pure formality without offering any guarantee. Just think of entry contracts and their clauses. Second, the framework of the directive leaves it unclear as to what processing operations can be justified solely based on the consent of the data subject. If no consent is given, the other legitimacy grounds in themselves seem to span the whole gamut of possibilities, unless one assumes that such consent legitimizes disproportionate and illegitimate processing—which is very questionable. It is tough to claim that such consent can legitimize a data processing operation of the government which exceeds its established authority. The same can be said when someone invokes the consent of a data subject to legitimize a totally disproportionate invasion of privacy. In penal law, the consent of a victim does not erase the criminal character of an action. Mandatory secrecy is not affected when a party gives consent to make something public. The mutual consent between parties on illegal agreements does not yield a legal agreement. As a result, the unambiguous consent of the data subjects is only one of the aspects that affects the considerations of the different interests. But it does not exclude that such given consent can tip the balance one way. At the same time, the true balance of power between the parties needs to be taken into account. If the freedom of choice is too limited, there can be no talk of voluntary consent. As a result, national legislators have to make it impossible that the consent criterion becomes absolute. Consent has to become part of a judicial balancing test. Finally, it is well advised that the withdrawal of consent should be explicitly mentioned in legislations.

Personal data have to be collected for "specified, explicit and legitimate purposes," Article 6 of the EC Directive stipulates.[10] This has to be established beforehand. Personal data should not be gathered at will. To the contrary, depending on the purpose of the processing operation, it should serve the established aim and not be excessive. It has to conform with the finality of the processing operation. Necessity, subsidiarity, and proportionality again take center stage. Not only must it be certain that the gathering of the information is necessary for reaching the purpose, but it also has to be established that there is no less intrusive way to achieve the result. In any case, the choice of data needs to be part of the considerations. Furthermore, the EC Directive insists on the accuracy and comprehensiveness of the personal data, which forces the processing party to update and correct information. Personal data cannot be stored beyond what is necessary to achieve the purpose of the processing operation.

Once the personal data have been collected, they cannot be processed in any way which is incompatible with the finality—the purpose—of the processing operation. The right to process personal data is recognized to strictly achieve the delineated and specified purposes. As soon as data are used for another purpose, it is unacceptable (unless it is part of another processing operation which meets all the conditions). The compatible use of data should be very strictly applied and is an extension of the principle of separation of processing operations. This is of the utmost importance, since it has become evident that transgressions of the purpose specification principle have caused the biggest problems in applying the existing rules. Obviously, the commercial and political exploitation of the existing processing operations is very tempting. Personal data have become a market product and there is plenty of interest from a great many corners. For example, student data contain information on diplomas and results. This information can be of strategic importance to direct marketing executives, publishers, producers of professional equipment, employers, temporary employment agencies, and so forth. Selling this information, however, is incompatible with the purpose of "student administration." If an educational institution wants to venture down this road and its statutes allow for the sale of such information, it will have to organize a separate processing operation which will again have to meet all the necessary requirements. Therefore, in the interest of privacy, a data processor does not have carte blanche with a broad or general processing right, but a limited and specified mandate. Incompatible use and diversion from the set purpose are issues as soon as a discrepancy can be established between the use of personal data and the finality for which the data were collected and processed.

Apart from the general rules on legitimacy of processing and the quality of data, data protection law also creates the rules of transparency and organizes the participation of the data subject in the control of the processing operation. These rules are already contained in the existing legislations and the EC Directive. They are interlinked. It is only because of the transparency of the processing operations that an individual can enforce proper controls and have a say on the use of his or her data.

There are two ways to ensure transparency. On the one hand, all data subjects, in the case that they don't already know so, need to be informed that their data are used in a processing operation. It has to happen immediately, whether the personal data are collected with the data subjects themselves or whether they are provided to the processor through a third party. The data subject at least has to be informed of the identity of the processing party and the purpose of the processing operation. It is desirable though that more information is provided about the rights of the data subjects: the fact that they are allowed to refuse giving their consent, the nature of the data which will be processed, third parties to which the data will be passed on, and so forth. This facilitates the assessment of legitimacy. On the other hand, each automated processing operation needs to be reported in all its aspects[11] to the supervisory authority, which must keep a public and accessible register. Such a register is essential to maintain overall control over the processing operations. The EC Directive, however, provides ample space for exemptions regarding the obligation of notification and the provision of information to the data subject. It is evident that this holds a danger for individual control and participation feasibility. Any diversion from the principle of full notification or information provision should be exceptional and carefully considered. Otherwise, the threat emerges again that the directive will be eroded.

The data subjects have the right of access and the right of rectification. They can investigate how the processing operation is carried out, what data bases exist, what their purpose is, who is responsible, and so forth.[12] If they discover incomplete or inaccurate, irrelevant, or outdated data, they can insist on rectification or erasure. But again, numerous exemptions are provided for. So here, too, national legislators should tread with extreme care and restraint. There may be good reasons to limit the access of data subjects to a processing operation (e.g., during a police investigation). Yet because of the pursued "high level of protection," such exemptions should be kept to a minimum. A good interim solution can be found in the indirect control mechanism when the supervisory authority acts in the name of the data subjects. The threshold to exercise the right to access and rectification should be kept as low as possible, calling for transparent procedures, low costs, as little formalism as possible, speed, and guidance. The individual has to be encouraged to take up his or her responsibility.

The data subject's right to object is of the utmost importance, certainly if his or her consent is used as a ground for legitimacy. If personal freedom is at the heart of the issue, the individuals must be able to decide for themselves whether the advantage of being part of the processing operation outweighs the dangers of an invasion of privacy. The EC Directive stipulates that, in the case of direct marketing, the effect of the data subject's objections should be immediate and automatic. That is good news. However, when it comes to other processing operations, the right to object is phrased much more cautiously. In Article 14 of the EC Directive such objections need "compelling legitimate grounds relating to his particular situation to the processing of data relating to him." In light of the catch-up operation to benefit privacy's freedom, this should be overturned. It would be better to say that objection is possible, unless the processor is legally obliged to process the information. Exemptions would only be granted if the processor proves that there are serious and justified reasons which necessitate the processing of the personal data. If privacy's freedom is taken seriously, it would mean that there would be a far-reaching protection of the individual's right to object. The power that emanates from data processing justifies that the individual's resistance always leads to legal mediation or a careful balancing of interests. The social values at stake far outstrip the administrative arguments. And as long as the powerful data processor fails to prove the contrary, the resistance of the data subject should prevail.

According to Article 15 of the EC Directive, every person has the right "not to be subject to a decision which produces legal effects concerning him or significantly affects him and which is based solely on automated processing of data." The article refers to automated processing of data "intended to evaluate certain personal aspects relating to him, such as his performance at work, creditworthiness, reliability, conduct, et cetera." The goal is to guarantee everyone's participation in important personal decisions. A dismissal based purely on the data from the company time clock is, as a result, unacceptable. It applies just as much to the rejection of a job seeker based on the results of a computerized psychotechnical assessment test or to a computerized job application package. Those decisions have to take professional experience or the result of a job interview into account. The automated test is insufficient, and it applies to such sectors as banking and insurance. The EU member states have to enact provisions which allow for the legal challenge of computerized decisions and which guarantee an individual's input in the decision-making procedures. Considering the dangers of further normalization and the further increase of controls, it is another essential reason to defend privacy's freedom. Everyone has to be free to be oneself and has to be able to express his or her personality fully. Decisions taken purely on the grounds of computerized comparisons of an individual with a stereotypical model have to be rejected out of hand. This is why the exemptions of Article 15 of the EC Directive have to be restricted as much as possible.[13]

From the start, data protection law has given rise to the creation of independent supervisory authorities—such as the *French Commission Nationale Informatique et Liberté*, the British Data Protection Register, and the Dutch Registratiekamer—which have, in the framework of the data protection law, taken several tasks upon them. Apart from keeping a processing register, they can, depending on national legislation, offer advice, investigate issues, handle complaints, take certain decisions on certain processing operations, provide authorizations, and take a case to court or even institute binding rules. Sometimes, they have far-reaching authority, as in the case of France's *Commission Nationale Informatique et Liberté*. Sometimes it has very limited impact, as in the case of Belgium's *Commission pour la Protection de la Vie Priveé*. The EC Directive does not change much, unless its implementation is used to change the powers of the supervisory bodies.[14] One needs to look beyond the authority granted to such supervisory institutions to make sure they can fully fulfill their task. They have to be able to give precedence to and function fully to compensate for the weakness and vulnerability of the data subjects. First and foremost, the supervisory institutions must be able to gain public trust. The data processors come at a later stage since they know very well how to protect their own interests. The raison d'être of such supervisory institutions is to compensate for the imbalance between the power of the data processors and the data subjects. This calls for a low entry threshold. Otherwise, the judicial branch would be sufficient. On the contrary, these supervisory authorities must not become inert, paralyzing roadblocks on the way to the courthouse. This takes courage and intellectual independence in the face of the government and economic interests. The institutions also need to be able to work in the right material conditions. Lack of manpower, reliance on volunteers, incompetence, cronyism, political appointments, and financial dependence may undermine their potential, credibility, strength, and independence.

The directive further stipulates that EU member states need to encourage professional organizations to set up codes of conduct under the umbrella of the supervisory authorities. These codes should seek to promote the application of the directive, taking into account the specific nature of some sectors. However, there is fear that sectoral self-regulatory initiatives will weaken guarantees, especially considering the hostile industry reaction to the EC Directive. On top of that, professional organizations represent primarily economic, not human right interests, raising the question of whether they have the right approach to handle the privacy issue. The array of possible exemptions within the directive might be used well outside their proper scope in codes of conduct.

Up to now, only the general rules of the EC Directive have come under review. But there is also a special procedure for the processing of sensitive information. Member states must ban the processing of "personal data revealing racial or ethnic origin, political opinions, religious or philosophical beliefs, trade-union membership, and the processing of data concerning health or sex life" (Article 8[1] of the EC Directive). In those cases, a fundamental data processing prohibition applies because it endangers not only privacy but also the principle of nondiscrimination. The special arrangement is important since it can counter the rise of neotribal ambitions: the lack of sensitive data makes it more difficult to include or exclude somebody from a group. All the more reason to be very strict on this issue. Yet this fundamental ban also allows for exemptions in a number of circumstances. For example, Article 8(4) of the EC Directive states that "subject to the provision of suitable safeguards, Member States may, for reasons of substantial public interest, lay down exemptions." There is even the provision for an exemption if the data subject has given "explicit consent" to the processing of such information. The objections raised earlier with regard to consent as grounds for legitimacy also apply now, but even more so, despite subtle but useless differences the EC Directive makes between "unambiguous" and "explicit" consent. One can only hope that national legislators will not be lured that easily in easing the special regimen for sensitive data. Here, too, the principle of consent needs to be kept at arm's length as much as possible.

The media have long known that privacy and the freedom of expression, both fundamental rights, do not mix well. This is evident when assessing the issue of personal data processing for journalistic purposes in the written and audiovisual media. Here we have two equal values in the balance. This has already led to claims in the media to fully withdraw the sector from the application of data processing law. This is the case in some national legislations, such as the Dutch Data Registration Act (1988). It makes any serious weighing and consideration of the different interests at stake impossible, even though the ECHR calls for such a balancing test. Even the media need to respect the limits of privacy, although every case has to be assessed differently, as mentioned in chapter 1. It cannot be said offhand that the freedom of press takes precedence over privacy's freedom, even when we disregard the different kinds of journalism or the changing news value of personal data. Even though their uneasy relationship cannot compare to that of privacy and marketing, it still has to be carefully balanced and any regulation on the processing of personal data cannot disregard this. The directive stipulates that a full exemption of the media is thus not desirable. This is a good thing. As a result, the EC Directive covers journalism in principle, but Article 9 forces member states to provide an exemption for the media. Based on consideration 37, member states shall provide for exemptions or derogations "necessary for the balance between fundamental rights as regards general measures on the legitimacy of data processing, measures on the transfer of data to third countries and the power of the supervisory authority." Certain competences a posteriori can be held on to, but it remains very much the question whether there should not be some built-in safeguards when it comes to sensitive information. A code of conduct in the sector appears to be imminent, even though past experiences with journalistic deontology leave something to be desired. Nevertheless, it is clear that it will be up to the judges to take up their constitutional and human rights responsibilities, because the tension between media and privacy has to be judged case by case in light of such elements as news value, the function of the people concerned, the nature of the published information, the way in which the information was obtained, etc.

The purpose of the directive is clearly stated in Article 1: "Member States shall neither restrict nor prohibit the free flow of personal data between Member States for reasons connected with" privacy protection. The harmonization of privacy protection at a "high level" of EU member state legislations removes every reason or pretense to intervene in the free flow of personal data. Within the European internal market, transborder traffic of personal data can freely flow. It can no longer be an argument that the free flow of personal data and the increase of exchanges as such are an increased threat, further endangering personal freedom. By relinquishing controls on transborder personal data flows, traffic further increases and develops, putting privacy under ever more pressure. It also becomes ever easier to move processing offshore, a move which should call for more control rather than fewer checks on data flows.

On top of that, the way in which the member states implement the directive is not as uniform as could be hoped for. Legislative differences will most probably soon emerge. The formal approval of a harmonized law will not have the same impact on reality in all the member states. Past experiences with data protection law already offer a cautionary tale and the phenomenon of symbolic legislation is not exceptional. The law in the books is often far removed from the law in action. Environmental legislation is living proof of that. There has to be a true political will to ensure the "high level" of privacy protection in day-to-day reality. Otherwise the national law will not be worth the paper it was written on. However, the mere existence of such legislation suffices for the EU legislator. As soon as every member state has a law in place, the transborder flow of personal data is free.

The transposition of the EC Directive into national legislation can create major differences. This does not only depend on the different political sensitivities in the EU member states (from laissez-faire to tight government control), but also on the bandwidth which it is granted. It is doubtful that a large measure of privacy protection is left at the lowest level. Alertness and a healthy dose of skepticism is called for. Legislators who are genuinely concerned about privacy have to keep reminding themselves that within the EU framework, privacy is not a goal in itself but is just taken along as necessary luggage. Also, they have to realize that data protection law is based on a dubious inversion of the onus of proof. Apart from the sensitive data regimen, personal data processing is legitimate until proof to the contrary is provided. That evidence has to be provided by or in name of the party which claims its privacy has been invaded. It is a system of a posteriori controls. On the other hand, and even though this system is preferable, there are strong feasibility arguments against the idea of an a priori control system which would be based, for example, on the granting of licenses.

The problematic inversion of the onus of proof justifies a strong implementation and enforcement of the new legislation. The proposed principles need to be implemented without any "flou artistique" or a slew of exemptions and derogations. The delineation of the set purpose and the separation of processing operations have to be carefully supervised. National legislators have to make sure that one processing operation fits one purpose, and that the finality is reasonably limited, because otherwise, the high level of protection will quickly be eroded. Such an implementation will automatically limit the processing authority which was granted, both at the level of quality (conformity) and use of personal data. The utmost reticence should be applied when it comes to accepting the data subject's consent as a basis for legitimacy: strict conditions should be set. Each time, the voluntary nature of the consent should be investigated while it should not totally predetermine the legitimacy of processing and still allow for a balancing of interests. Finally, the data subject's consent should not be absolute. A processing operation which disproportionately invades privacy must still be able to be considered illegal, even if prior consent is given. On the other hand, the right to object must be expanded to cover all processing operations, exempting only those prescribed by law. It should be up to the processors to prove that they have serious enough reasons to legitimize the processing despite the objections of the data subject. The individual's right to object should be free and easy to express. Limits on the right of information, access and rectification, and a more flexible notification system will erode the principle of transparency which is crucial to both the involvement of the data subject and a posteriori controls. They have to be avoided. Finally, the supervisory authority needs to be truly independent and pack a forceful punch. This implies a strong stand on privacy as well as sizable financial backing.

In short, it will not be easy to make a virtue of necessity. The ambiguity is too pervasive and social developments have already taken too big a lead. Privacy resistance of the 1960s and 1970s, which based itself on the foundations of the democratic constitutional state to safely channel the efficiency and information dream, has not won its fight. Instead of a fundamental reflection on the further development of our society, an ambiguous arrangement emerged, in which privacy had to make way for "data protection," in which invasions of privacy are legitimized, even though it is conditional. One can only hope that policymakers, politicians in charge, and individuals sufficiently realize what the problem is and try to make the best of it. Otherwise, the future of personal freedom looks bleak.

Notes

1. There are exceptions. The success of the personal computer, for example, was not directly linked to the development of the microprocessor. To the contrary, it is the result of the hijacking, or reinterpretation, of existing technical possibilities, by a few people in the rebellious Silicon Valley of the 1970s. They developed personal computers hoping to contribute to the liberation of humankind. It happened, even though big business had other purposes in mind for computers. A typical example is the garage tale of Steve Jobs and Steve Wozniac, who created Apple together as a producer of alternative information technology. Afterward, they became part of big business just as well. Some aspects of the Internet possibly give us another example: more free speech; easier, cheaper, and more controllable (?) communication. Hackers and their clubs can probably be seen as an illustration of the resistance that computers can exude (the Robin Hoods of the ignorant).

2. The OECD Guidelines offer eight core principles of personal data protection (cf. Art. 7–14 of the OECD Guidelines). They are:

1) the *collection limitation principle*, limiting the collection of personal data and stating that any such data should be obtained by lawful and fair means and, where appropriate, with the knowledge or consent of the data subject (= *the fairness principle*); 2) the *data quality principle*, which says personal data should be relevant to the purposes for which they are to be used, and, to the extent necessary for those purposes, should be accurate, complete, and kept up-to-date; 3) the *purpose specification principle*, which says the purposes for which personal data are collected, processed, and used should be specified and the subsequent use limited to the fulfillment of those purposes; 4) the *use limitation principle*, stating that personal data should not be disclosed, made available, or otherwise used unless there is consent of the data subject; or by the authority of law; 5) *the security safeguards principle*, saying that personal data should be protected by reasonable security safeguards against such risks as loss or unauthorized access, destruction, use, modification, or disclosure of data; 6) the *openness principle*, stipulating that there should be a general policy of openness about developments, practices, and policies, means should be readily available of establishing the existence and nature of personal data, and the main purposes of their use, as well as the identity and usual residence of the data controller; 7) the *individual participation principle*, giving individuals the right to locate, check, erase, rectify, or complete data; and 8) the *accountability principle*, saying that the data controller should be accountable for complying with the principles.

3. Art. 5 of Convention 108 stipulates that "Personal data undergoing automatic processing shall be

a) obtained and processed fairly and lawfully (the *fairness principle*); b) stored for specified and legitimate purposes and not used in a way incompatible with those purposes (the *purpose specification principle* or *finality principle*, including the *legiti-*

macy principle); c) adequate, relevant and not excessive in relation to the purposes for which they are stored; d) accurate and, where necessary, kept up to date (*data quality principle*); and e) preserved in a form which permits identification of the data subjects for no longer than is required for the purpose for which those data are stored (*time limitation principle*).

Art. 6 stipulates that personal data revealing racial origin, political opinions, or religious or other beliefs, as well as personal data concerning health or sexual life, may not be processed automatically unless domestic law provides appropriate safeguards (*collection limitation principle*). Art. 7 centers on the *security safeguards principle*, calling for security measures to protect "personal data stored in automated data files against accidental or unauthorized destruction or accidental loss as well as against unauthorized access, alteration, or dissemination." Art. 8a incorporates the *openness principle* and the *accountability principle* by stipulating that any person should be able to establish the existence of an automated personal data file, its main purposes, as well as the identity and habitual residence or principal place of business of the controller of the file. Sections b and c meet the concerns of the *individual participation principle*: the data subject has the right to access and rectification.

4. The mere idea of "the privacy of a legal person" is simply absurd, if only because a legal person is never free, but always bound by its articles of association. But even in a legal, theoretical, and ethical sense, it is out of place, and even cynical, to transpose the essential freedom of an individual on abstract entities which have no reason to be beyond the purpose given to them by others. It is beyond doubt that commercial and company secrets need to be respected, but this is an issue that has nothing to do with privacy. Privacy of legal persons is demagogic nonsense. The fact alone that it is being considered that data protection should also apply to corporate bodies probably shows that for some people personal data processing has precious little to do with their privacy.

5. Cf. the fairness principle of the OECD Guidelines and Treaty 108.

6. This is in line with the principle contained in labor law which requires negotiations between employers and the workforce whenever employers want to use employment data or install new surveillance equipment on the work floor. Cf. Council of Europe, Council of Ministers, Recommendation No. R (89) 2 of the Committee of Ministers to Member States on the Protection of Data used for Employment Purposes, Adopted by the Committee of Ministers, on 18 January 1989, p. 5.

7. Cf. Art. 6 of the EC Directive: "1. Member States shall provide that personal data must be:

(a) processed fairly and lawfully; (b) *collected for specified, explicit and legitimate purposes and not further processed in a way incompatible with those purposes.* Further processing of data for historical, statistical or scientific purposes shall not be considered as incompatible provided that Member States provide appropriate safeguards; (c) adequate, relevant and not excessive in relation to the purposes for which they are collected and/or further processed; (d) accurate and, where necessary, kept up to date; every reasonable step must be taken to ensure that data which are inaccurate or incomplete, having regard to the purposes for which they were collected or for which they are further processed, are erased or rectified; (e) kept in a form which permits identification of data subjects for no longer than is necessary for the purposes for which the data were collected or for which they are further processed.

Member States shall lay down appropriate safeguards for personal data stored for longer periods for historical, statistical or scientific use; 2. It shall be for the controller to ensure that paragraph 1 is complied with."

8. Specifically when "(b) processing is necessary for the performance of a contract to which the data subject is party or in order to take steps at the request of the data subject prior to entering into a contract; or (c) processing is necessary for compliance with a legal obligation to which the controller is subject; or (d) processing is necessary in order to protect the vital interests of the data subject" (Art. 7 of the EC Directive).

9. In this case, the processing is only acceptable if it is "necessary for the performance of a task carried out in the public interest or in the exercise of official authority vested in the controller or in a third party to whom the data are disclosed" (Art. 7 [e] of the EC Directive). This does not address situations in which public interest and law and order tasks are executed by private persons.

10. See Art. 6 of the EC Directive, supra footnote 7.

11. Art. 19 of the EC Directive: "Member States shall specify the information to be given in the notification. It shall include at least: (a) the name and address of the controller and of his representative, if any; (b) the purpose or purposes of the processing; (c) a description of the category or categories of data subject and of the data or categories of data relating to them; (d) the recipients or categories of recipient to whom the data might be disclosed; (e) proposed transfers of data to third countries; (f) a general description allowing a preliminary assessment to be made of the appropriateness of the measures taken pursuant to Article 17 to ensure security of processing."

12. Art. 12 of the EC Directive: "Member States shall guarantee every data right to obtain from the controller:

(a) without constraint at reasonable intervals and without excessive delay or expense: confirmation as to whether or not data relating to him are being processed and information at least as to the purposes of the processing, the categories of data concerned, and the recipients or categories of recipients to whom the data are disclosed, communication to him in an intelligible form of the data undergoing processing and of any available information as to their source, knowledge of the logic involved in any automatic processing of data concerning him at least in the case of the automated decisions referred to in Article 15 (1); (b) as appropriate the rectification, erasure or blocking of data the processing of which does not comply with the provisions of this Directive, in particular because of the incomplete or inaccurate nature of the data; (c) notification to third parties to whom the data have been disclosed of any rectification, erasure or blocking carried out in compliance with (b), unless this proves impossible or involves a disproportionate effort."

13. Member states are allowed to grant exemptions on the ban on computerized individual decisions if such a decision "(a) is taken in the course of the entering into or performance of a contract, provided the request for the entering into or the performance of the contract, lodged by the data subject, has been satisfied or that there are suitable measures to safeguard his legitimate interests, such as arrangements allowing him to put his point of view; or (b) is authorized by a law which also lays down measures to safeguard the data subject's legitimate interests."

14. Some member states, however, will have to expand the authority of the existing institutions, including the preparatory inquiry into processing which involves specific risks for the individual rights and freedoms. One can envisage processing which uses an interchangeable identification number or processing which the supervisory institutions consider especially risky.

∞

Conclusion

In Western democratic societies, privacy is the concept that embodies individual freedom. As such, privacy touches the foundations of our project of society. It is the reason privacy has an impact on a whole range of situations. This is why privacy is elusive and has to remain so. This is why privacy is contextual, relational, and relative. This is why privacy is never absolute.

Privacy is preeminently social and thrives on interhuman tensions. For Robinson Crusoe, privacy was an empty concept until Friday's arrival. Without society, personal freedom makes no sense. It also works the other way around. A prisoner in solitary confinement has no privacy, much like Orwell's Winston Smith. Kafka's Joseph K., too, totally exposed by an opaque system, has lost all freedom. Totalitarianism in all its guises is incompatible with any form of privacy. Absolute power, whatever its appearance, destroys resistance and freedom. Privacy can only survive in a system where freedom and resistance to power are respected.

This is an essential theme for a society which wants a maximum of individual freedom to function as much as possible as a unity. Such a society has to walk a tightrope at all levels. Permanent mediation is necessary to simultaneously safeguard individual freedom and the common project. Privacy is always in the balance with the public interest and the freedoms and rights of others. This tension should never disappear and the balance should never be replaced by an ax. There are no values, whether they be economic, religious, scientific, ethical, political, tribal, or whatever, which take absolute priority over personal freedom. Otherwise, the world is turning a murky shade of gray with its deadening uniformity of totalitarianism and the endless monotony of the lowest common denominator. Unfortunately, these dangers always lurk just below the surface. Forces of many origins threaten to reduce privacy to a shadow of its former self. Sometimes this even happens under the guise of privacy itself, casting a further pall over the issue. Only the calls for a true and open experience of personal freedom are worthy of the name "privacy."

People come in all sizes and shapes and it takes a lot of wriggling before they fit inside the models of conformity. A pluralist society fortunately recognizes the principle of resistance and the fact that individual behavior cannot be molded or steered at will. It glorifies the opposite of monotony and thus has to protect diversity, color, movement, and discussion, and to value freedom and cross-fertilization against any form of behavioral steering, whatever the driving force behind it, its arguments, or its means. Individuals are free to be and become what they choose, free to be different, free to determine behavior, free to choose a social personality, free to interact with others, free to choose a path in life, and so on. This is what's at stake for emancipatory privacy. It is privacy's freedom.[1]

Note

1. To improve the readability of this book, it contains few references to other authors. The bibliography includes a succinct overview of the literature which has been consulted. Obviously, some have had a greater impact on this book than others—which is why I would specifically like to mention the work of René Foqué, August 't Hart, and François Rigaux, as well as my long, friendly, and fruitful cooperation with Paul De Hert.

...ntifiable natural person ("data subject"); an identifiable person is one ...o can be identified, directly or indirectly, in particular by reference ...an identification number or to one or more factors specific to his ...ysical, physiological, mental, economic, cultural or social identity;
...ocessing of personal data" ("processing") shall mean any operation ...set of operations which is performed upon personal data, whether ...not by automatic means, such as collection, recording, organization, ...rage, adaptation or alteration, retrieval, consultation, use, disclosure ...transmission, dissemination or otherwise making available, alignment ...combination, blocking, erasure or destruction;
...ersonal data filing system" ("filing system") shall mean any structured ...t of personal data which are accessible according to specific criteria, ...hether centralized, decentralized or dispersed on a functional or geo-...raphical basis;
...controller" shall mean the natural or legal person, public authority, ...gency or any other body which alone or jointly with others determines ...he purposes and means of the processing of personal data; where the ...urposes and means of processing are determined by national or Com-...nunity laws or regulations, the controller or the specific criteria for his ...nomination may be designated by national or Community law;
...'processor" shall mean a natural or legal person, public authority, ...agency or any other body which processes personal data on behalf of the ...controller;
"third party" shall mean any natural or legal person, public authority, agency or any other body other than the data subject, the controller, the processor and the persons who, under the direct authority of the controller or the processor, are authorized to process the data;
"recipient" shall mean a natural or legal person, public authority, agency or any other body to whom data are disclosed, whether a third party or not; however, authorities which may receive data in the framework of a particular inquiry shall not be regarded as recipients;
"the data subject's consent" shall mean any freely given specific and informed indication of his wishes by which the data subject signifies his agreement to personal data relating to him being processed.

Article 3

Scope

This Directive shall apply to the processing of personal data wholly or partly by automatic means, and to the processing otherwise than by auto-

∞

Appendix

Directive 95/46/EC of the European Parliament and of the Council

On the protection of individuals with regard to the process
data and on the free movement of such data.

24 October 1995

Chapter I: General Provisions

Article 1
Object of the Directive
1. In accordance with this Directive, Member States shall protec
   mental rights and freedoms of natural persons, and in part
   right to privacy with respect to the processing of personal dat
2. Member States shall neither restrict nor prohibit the free flow
   data between Member States for reasons connected with the
   afforded under paragraph 1.

Article 2
Definitions
For the purposes of this Directive:
(a) "personal data" shall mean any information relating to an ider

matic means of personal data which form part of a filing system or are intended to form part of a filing system.

2. This Directive shall not apply to the processing of personal data:

—in the course of an activity which falls outside the scope of Community law, such as those provided for by Titles V and VI of the Treaty on European Union and in any case to processing operations concerning public security, defence, State security (including the economic well-being of the State when the processing operation relates to State security matters) and the activities of the State in areas of criminal law,

—by a natural person in the course of a purely personal or household activity.

Article 4
National law applicable

1. Each Member State shall apply the national provisions it adopts pursuant to this Directive to the processing of personal data where:

   (a) the processing is carried out in the context of the activities of an establishment of the controller on the territory of the Member State; when the same controller is established on the territory of several Member States, he must take the necessary measures to ensure that each of these establishments complies with the obligations laid down by the national law applicable;

   (b) the controller is not established on the Member State's territory, but in a place where its national law applies by virtue of international public law;

   (c) the controller is not established on Community territory and, for purposes of processing personal data makes use of equipment, automated or otherwise, situated on the territory of the said Member State, unless such equipment is used only for purposes of transit through the territory of the Community.

2. In the circumstances referred to in paragraph 1 (c), the controller must designate a representative established in the territory of that Member State, without prejudice to legal actions which could be initiated against the controller himself.

Chapter II: General Rules on the Lawfulness of the Processing of Personal Data

Article 5
Member States shall, within the limits of the provisions of this Chapter, determine more precisely the conditions under which the processing of personal data is lawful.

SECTION I: PRINCIPLES RELATING
TO DATA QUALITY

Article 6
1. Member States shall provide that personal data must be:
   (a) processed fairly and lawfully;
   (b) collected for specified, explicit and legitimate purposes and not further processed in a way incompatible with those purposes. Further processing of data for historical, statistical or scientific purposes shall not be considered as incompatible provided that Member States provide appropriate safeguards;
   (c) adequate, relevant and not excessive in relation to the purposes for which they are collected and/or further processed;
   (d) accurate and, where necessary, kept up to date; every reasonable step must be taken to ensure that data which are inaccurate or incomplete, having regard to the purposes for which they were collected or for which they are further processed, are erased or rectified;
   (e) kept in a form which permits identification of data subjects for no longer than is necessary for the purposes for which the data were collected or for which they are further processed. Member States shall lay down appropriate safeguards for personal data stored for longer periods for historical, statistical or scientific use.
2. It shall be for the controller to ensure that paragraph 1 is complied with.

SECTION II: CRITERIA FOR MAKING DATA
PROCESSING LEGITIMATE

Article 7
Member States shall provide that personal data may be processed only if:
(a) the data subject has unambiguously given his consent; or
(b) processing is necessary for the performance of a contract to which the data subject is party or in order to take steps at the request of the data subject prior to entering into a contract; or
(c) processing is necessary for compliance with a legal obligation to which the controller is subject; or
(d) processing is necessary in order to protect the vital interests of the data subject; or

(e) processing is necessary for the performance of a task carried out in the public interest or in the exercise of official authority vested in the controller or in a third party to whom the data are disclosed; or

(f) processing is necessary for the purposes of the legitimate interests pursued by the controller or by the third party or parties to whom the data are disclosed, except where such interests are overridden by the interests for fundamental rights and freedoms of the data subject which require protection under Article 1 (1).

SECTION III: SPECIAL CATEGORIES OF PROCESSING

Article 8
The processing of special categories of data

1. Member States shall prohibit the processing of personal data revealing racial or ethnic origin, political opinions, religious or philosophical beliefs, trade-union membership, and the processing of data concerning health or sex life.

2. Paragraph 1 shall not apply where:

   (a) the data subject has given his explicit consent to the processing of those data, except where the laws of the Member State provide that the prohibition referred to in paragraph 1 may not be lifted by the data subject's giving his consent; or

   (b) processing is necessary for the purposes of carrying out the obligations and specific rights of the controller in the field of employment law in so far as it is authorized by national law providing for adequate safeguards; or

   (c) processing is necessary to protect the vital interests of the data subject or of another person where the data subject is physically or legally incapable of giving his consent; or

   (d) processing is carried out in the course of its legitimate activities with appropriate guarantees by a foundation, association or any other non-profit-seeking body with a political, philosophical, religious or trade-union aim and on condition that the processing relates solely to the members of the body or to persons who have regular contact with it in connection with its purposes and that the data are not disclosed to a third party without the consent of the data subjects; or

(e) the processing relates to data which are manifestly made public by the data subject or is necessary for the establishment, exercise or defence of legal claims.

3. Paragraph 1 shall not apply where processing of the data is required for the purposes of preventive medicine, medical diagnosis, the provision of care or treatment or the management of health-care services, and where those data are processed by a health professional subject under national law or rules established by national competent bodies to the obligation of professional secrecy or by another person also subject to an equivalent obligation of secrecy.

4. Subject to the provision of suitable safeguards, Member States may, for reasons of substantial public interest, lay down exemptions in addition to those laid down in paragraph 2 either by national law or by decision of the supervisory authority.

5. Processing of data relating to offences, criminal convictions or security measures may be carried out only under the control of official authority, or if suitable specific safeguards are provided under national law, subject to derogations which may be granted by the Member State under national provisions providing suitable specific safeguards. However, a complete register of criminal convictions may be kept only under the control of official authority.

Member States may provide that data relating to administrative sanctions or judgements in civil cases shall also be processed under the control of official authority.

6. Derogations from paragraph 1 provided for in paragraphs 4 and 5 shall be notified to the Commission.

7. Member States shall determine the conditions under which a national identification number or any other identifier of general application may be processed.

Article 9
Processing of personal data and freedom of expression
Member States shall provide for exemptions or derogations from the provisions of this Chapter, Chapter IV and Chapter VI for the processing of personal data carried out solely for journalistic purposes or the purpose of artistic or literary expression only if they are necessary to reconcile the right to privacy with the rules governing freedom of expression.

SECTION IV: INFORMATION TO BE GIVEN
TO THE DATA SUBJECT

Article 10
Information in cases of collection of data from the data subject
Member States shall provide that the controller or his representative must provide a data subject from whom data relating to himself are collected with at least the following information, except where he already has it:
(a) the identity of the controller and of his representative, if any;
(b) the purposes of the processing for which the data are intended;
(c) any further information such as
  —the recipients or categories of recipients of the data,
  —whether replies to the questions are obligatory or voluntary, as well as the possible consequences of failure to reply,
  —the existence of the right of access to and the right to rectify the data concerning him
  in so far as such further information is necessary, having regard to the specific circumstances in which the data are collected, to guarantee fair processing in respect of the data subject.

Article 11
Information where the data have not been obtained from the data subject
1. Where the data have not been obtained from the data subject, Member States shall provide that the controller or his representative must at the time of undertaking the recording of personal data or if a disclosure to a third party is envisaged, no later than the time when the data are first disclosed provide the data subject with at least the following information, except where he already has it:
(a) the identity of the controller and of his representative, if any;
(b) the purposes of the processing;
(c) any further information such as
  —the categories of data concerned,
  —the recipients or categories of recipients,
  —the existence of the right of access to and the right to rectify the data concerning him
  in so far as such further information is necessary, having regard to the specific circumstances in which the data are processed, to guarantee fair processing in respect of the data subject.

2. Paragraph 1 shall not apply where, in particular for processing for statistical purposes or for the purposes of historical or scientific research, the provision of such information proves impossible or would involve a disproportionate effort or if recording or disclosure is expressly laid down by law. In these cases Member States shall provide appropriate safeguards.

SECTION V: THE DATA SUBJECT'S RIGHT OF ACCESS TO DATA

Article 12
Right of access
Member States shall guarantee every data subject the right to obtain from the controller:

(a) without constraint at reasonable intervals and without excessive delay or expense:
—confirmation as to whether or not data relating to him are being processed and information at least as to the purposes of the processing, the categories of data concerned, and the recipients or categories of recipients to whom the data are disclosed,
—communication to him in an intelligible form of the data undergoing processing and of any available information as to their source,
—knowledge of the logic involved in any automatic processing of data concerning him at least in the case of the automated decisions referred to in Article 15 (1);

(b) as appropriate the rectification, erasure or blocking of data the processing of which does not comply with the provisions of this Directive, in particular because of the incomplete or inaccurate nature of the data;

(c) notification to third parties to whom the data have been disclosed of any rectification, erasure or blocking carried out in compliance with (b), unless this proves impossible or involves a disproportionate effort.

SECTION VI: EXEMPTIONS AND RESTRICTIONS

Article 13
Exemptions and restrictions
1. Member States may adopt legislative measures to restrict the scope of the obligations and rights provided for in Articles 6 (1), 10, 11 (1),

12 and 21 when such a restriction constitutes a necessary measure to safeguard:

(a) national security;

(b) defence;

(c) public security;

(d) the prevention, investigation, detection and prosecution of criminal offences, or of breaches of ethics for regulated professions;

(e) an important economic or financial interest of a Member State or of the European Union, including monetary, budgetary and taxation matters;

(f) a monitoring, inspection or regulatory function connected, even occasionally, with the exercise of official authority in cases referred to in (c), (d) and (e);

(g) the protection of the data subject or of the rights and freedoms of others.

2. Subject to adequate legal safeguards, in particular that the data are not used for taking measures or decisions regarding any particular individual, Member States may, where there is clearly no risk of breaching the privacy of the data subject, restrict by a legislative measure the rights provided for in Article 12 when data are processed solely for purposes of scientific research or are kept in personal form for a period which does not exceed the period necessary for the sole purpose of creating statistics.

SECTION VII: THE DATA SUBJECT'S RIGHT TO OBJECT

Article 14

The data subject's right to object

Member States shall grant the data subject the right:

(a) at least in the cases referred to in Article 7 (e) and (f), to object at any time on compelling legitimate grounds relating to his particular situation to the processing of data relating to him, save where otherwise provided by national legislation. Where there is a justified objection, the processing instigated by the controller may no longer involve those data;

(b) to object, on request and free of charge, to the processing of personal data relating to him which the controller anticipates being processed for the purposes of direct marketing, or to be informed before personal data are disclosed for the first time to third parties or used on their behalf for the purposes of direct marketing, and to be expressly offered the right to object free of charge to such disclosures or uses.

Member States shall take the necessary measures to ensure that data subjects are aware of the existence of the right referred to in the first subparagraph of (b).

Article 15
Automated individual decisions
1. Member States shall grant the right to every person not to be subject to a decision which produces legal effects concerning him or significantly affects him and which is based solely on automated processing of data intended to evaluate certain personal aspects relating to him, such as his performance at work, creditworthiness, reliability, conduct, etc.
2. Subject to the other Articles of this Directive, Member States shall provide that a person may be subjected to a decision of the kind referred to in paragraph 1 if that decision:
   (a) is taken in the course of the entering into or performance of a contract, provided the request for the entering into or the performance of the contract, lodged by the data subject, has been satisfied or that there are suitable measures to safeguard his legitimate interests, such as arrangements allowing him to put his point of view; or
   (b) is authorized by a law which also lays down measures to safeguard the data subject's legitimate interests.

SECTION VIII: CONFIDENTIALITY AND SECURITY OF PROCESSING

Article 16
Confidentiality of processing
Any person acting under the authority of the controller or of the processor, including the processor himself, who has access to personal data must not process them except on instructions from the controller, unless he is required to do so by law.

Article 17
Security of processing
1. Member States shall provide that the controller must implement appropriate technical and organizational measures to protect personal data

against accidental or unlawful destruction or accidental loss, alteration, unauthorized disclosure or access, in particular where the processing involves the transmission of data over a network, and against all other unlawful forms of processing.

Having regard to the state of the art and the cost of their implementation, such measures shall ensure a level of security appropriate to the risks represented by the processing and the nature of the data to be protected.

2. The Member States shall provide that the controller must, where processing is carried out on his behalf, choose a processor providing sufficient guarantees in respect of the technical security measures and organizational measures governing the processing to be carried out, and must ensure compliance with those measures.

3. The carrying out of processing by way of a processor must be governed by a contract or legal act binding the processor to the controller and stipulating in particular that:
—the processor shall act only on instructions from the controller,
—the obligations set out in paragraph 1, as defined by the law of the Member State in which the processor is established, shall also be incumbent on the processor.

4. For the purposes of keeping proof, the parts of the contract or the legal act relating to data protection and the requirements relating to the measures referred to in paragraph 1 shall be in writing or in another equivalent form.

SECTION IX: NOTIFICATION

Article 18
Obligation to notify the supervisory authority

1. Member States shall provide that the controller or his representative, if any, must notify the supervisory authority referred to in Article 28 before carrying out any wholly or partly automatic processing operation or set of such operations intended to serve a single purpose or several related purposes.

2. Member States may provide for the simplification of or exemption from notification only in the following cases and under the following conditions:
—where, for categories of processing operations which are unlikely, taking account of the data to be processed, to affect adversely the rights and

freedoms of data subjects, they specify the purposes of the processing, the data or categories of data undergoing processing, the category or categories of data subject, the recipients or categories of recipient to whom the data are to be disclosed and the length of time the data are to be stored, and/or
—where the controller, in compliance with the national law which governs him, appoints a personal data protection official, responsible in particular:
—for ensuring in an independent manner the internal application of the national provisions taken pursuant to this Directive
—for keeping the register of processing operations carried out by the controller, containing the items of information referred to in Article 21 (2), thereby ensuring that the rights and freedoms of the data subjects are unlikely to be adversely affected by the processing operations.

3. Member States may provide that paragraph 1 does not apply to processing whose sole purpose is the keeping of a register which according to laws or regulations is intended to provide information to the public and which is open to consultation either by the public in general or by any person demonstrating a legitimate interest.

4. Member States may provide for an exemption from the obligation to notify or a simplification of the notification in the case of processing operations referred to in Article 8 (2) (d).

5. Member States may stipulate that certain or all nonautomatic processing operations involving personal data shall be notified, or provide for these processing operations to be subject to simplified notification.

Article 19
Contents of notification
1. Member States shall specify the information to be given in the notification. It shall include at least:
   (a) the name and address of the controller and of his representative, if any;
   (b) the purpose or purposes of the processing;
   (c) a description of the category or categories of data subject and of the data or categories of data relating to them;
   (d) the recipients or categories of recipient to whom the data might be disclosed;
   (e) proposed transfers of data to third countries;
   (f) a general description allowing a preliminary assessment to be made

of the appropriateness of the measures taken pursuant to Article 17 to ensure security of processing.
2. Member States shall specify the procedures under which any change affecting the information referred to in paragraph 1 must be notified to the supervisory authority.

Article 20
Prior checking
1. Member States shall determine the processing operations likely to present specific risks to the rights and freedoms of data subjects and shall check that these processing operations are examined prior to the start thereof.
2. Such prior checks shall be carried out by the supervisory authority following receipt of a notification from the controller or by the data protection official, who, in cases of doubt, must consult the supervisory authority.
3. Member States may also carry out such checks in the context of preparation either of a measure of the national parliament or of a measure based on such a legislative measure, which define the nature of the processing and lay down appropriate safeguards.

Article 21
Publicizing of processing operations
1. Member States shall take measures to ensure that processing operations are publicized.
2. Member States shall provide that a register of processing operations notified in accordance with Article 18 shall be kept by the supervisory authority.
The register shall contain at least the information listed in Article 19 (1) (a) to (e).
The register may be inspected by any person.
3. Member States shall provide, in relation to processing operations not subject to notification, that controllers or another body appointed by the Member States make available at least the information referred to in Article 19 (1) (a) to (e) in an appropriate form to any person on request.
Member States may provide that this provision does not apply to processing whose sole purpose is the keeping of a register which according to laws or regulations is intended to provide information to the public and which is open to consultation either by the public in general or by any person who can provide proof of a legitimate interest.

Chapter III: Judicial Remedies, Liabilities, and Sanctions

Article 22
Remedies
Without prejudice to any administrative remedy for which provision may be made, inter alia before the supervisory authority referred to in Article 28, prior to referral to the judicial authority, Member States shall provide for the right of every person to a judicial remedy for any breach of the rights guaranteed him by the national law applicable to the processing in question.

Article 23
Liability
1. Member States shall provide that any person who has suffered damage as a result of an unlawful processing operation or of any act incompatible with the national provisions adopted pursuant to this Directive is entitled to receive compensation from the controller for the damage suffered.
2. The controller may be exempted from this liability, in whole or in part, if he proves that he is not responsible for the event giving rise to the damage.

Article 24
Sanctions
The Member States shall adopt suitable measures to ensure the full implementation of the provisions of this Directive and shall in particular lay down the sanctions to be imposed in case of infringement of the provisions adopted pursuant to this Directive.

Chapter IV: Transfer of Personal Data to Third Countries

Article 25
Principles
1. The Member States shall provide that the transfer to a third country of personal data which are undergoing processing or are intended for processing after transfer may take place only if, without prejudice to compliance with the national provisions adopted pursuant to the other

provisions of this Directive, the third country in question ensures an adequate level of protection.

2. The adequacy of the level of protection afforded by a third country shall be assessed in the light of all the circumstances surrounding a data transfer operation or set of data transfer operations; particular consideration shall be given to the nature of the data, the purpose and duration of the proposed processing operation or operations, the country of origin and country of final destination, the rules of law, both general and sectoral, in force in the third country in question and the professional rules and security measures which are complied with in that country.

3. The Member States and the Commission shall inform each other of cases where they consider that a third country does not ensure an adequate level of protection within the meaning of paragraph 2.

4. Where the Commission finds, under the procedure provided for in Article 31 (2), that a third country does not ensure an adequate level of protection within the meaning of paragraph 2 of this Article, Member States shall take the measures necessary to prevent any transfer of data of the same type to the third country in question.

5. At the appropriate time, the Commission shall enter into negotiations with a view to remedying the situation resulting from the finding made pursuant to paragraph 4.

6. The Commission may find, in accordance with the procedure referred to in Article 31 (2), that a third country ensures an adequate level of protection within the meaning of paragraph 2 of this Article, by reason of its domestic law or of the international commitments it has entered into, particularly upon conclusion of the negotiations referred to in paragraph 5, for the protection of the private lives and basic freedoms and rights of individuals.

   Member States shall take the measures necessary to comply with the Commission's decision.

Article 26

Derogations

1. By way of derogation from Article 25 and save where otherwise provided by domestic law governing particular cases, Member States shall provide that a transfer or a set of transfers of personal data to a third country which does not ensure an adequate level of protection within the meaning of Article 25 (2) may take place on condition that:

(a) the data subject has given his consent unambiguously to the proposed transfer; or

(b) the transfer is necessary for the performance of a contract between the data subject and the controller or the implementation of precontractual measures taken in response to the data subject's request; or

(c) the transfer is necessary for the conclusion or performance of a contract concluded in the interest of the data subject between the controller and a third party; or

(d) the transfer is necessary or legally required on important public interest grounds, or for the establishment, exercise or defence of legal claims; or

(e) the transfer is necessary in order to protect the vital interests of the data subject; or

(f) the transfer is made from a register which according to laws or regulations is intended to provide information to the public and which is open to consultation either by the public in general or by any person who can demonstrate legitimate interest, to the extent that the conditions laid down in law for consultation are fulfilled in the particular case.

2. Without prejudice to paragraph 1, a Member State may authorize a transfer or a set of transfers of personal data to a third country which does not ensure an adequate level of protection within the meaning of Article 25 (2), where the controller adduces adequate safeguards with respect to the protection of the privacy and fundamental rights and freedoms of individuals and as regards the exercise of the corresponding rights; such safeguards may in particular result from appropriate contractual clauses.

3. The Member State shall inform the Commission and the other Member States of the authorizations it grants pursuant to paragraph 2.

If a Member State or the Commission objects on justified grounds involving the protection of the privacy and fundamental rights and freedoms of individuals, the Commission shall take appropriate measures in accordance with the procedure laid down in Article 31 (2).

Member States shall take the necessary measures to comply with the Commission's decision.

4. Where the Commission decides, in accordance with the procedure referred to in Article 31 (2), that certain standard contractual clauses offer sufficient safeguards as required by paragraph 2, Member States shall take the necessary measures to comply with the Commission's decision.

Chapter V: Codes of Conduct

Article 27
1. The Member States and the Commission shall encourage the drawing up of codes of conduct intended to contribute to the proper implementation of the national provisions adopted by the Member States pursuant to this Directive, taking account of the specific features of the various sectors.
2. Member States shall make provision for trade associations and other bodies representing other categories of controllers which have drawn up draft national codes or which have the intention of amending or extending existing national codes to be able to submit them to the opinion of the national authority.
   Member States shall make provision for this authority to ascertain, among other things, whether the drafts submitted to it are in accordance with the national provisions adopted pursuant to this Directive. If it sees fit, the authority shall seek the views of data subjects or their representatives.
3. Draft Community codes, and amendments or extensions to existing Community codes, may be submitted to the Working Party referred to in Article 29. This Working Party shall determine, among other things, whether the drafts submitted to it are in accordance with the national provisions adopted pursuant to this Directive. If it sees fit, the authority shall seek the views of data subjects or their representatives. The Commission may ensure appropriate publicity for the codes which have been approved by the Working Party.

Chapter VI: Supervisory Authority and Working Party on the Protection of Individuals with Regard to the Processing of Personal Data

Article 28
Supervisory authority
1. Each Member State shall provide that one or more public authorities are responsible for monitoring the application within its territory of the provisions adopted by the Member States pursuant to this Directive.
   These authorities shall act with complete independence in exercising the functions entrusted to them.
2. Each Member State shall provide that the supervisory authorities are consulted when drawing up administrative measures or regulations relating

to the protection of individuals' rights and freedoms with regard to the processing of personal data.

3. Each authority shall in particular be endowed with:

—investigative powers, such as powers of access to data forming the subject-matter of processing operations and powers to collect all the information necessary for the performance of its supervisory duties,

—effective powers of intervention, such as, for example, that of delivering opinions before processing operations are carried out, in accordance with Article 20, and ensuring appropriate publication of such opinions, of ordering the blocking, erasure or destruction of data, of imposing a temporary or definitive ban on processing, of warning or admonishing the controller, or that of referring the matter to national parliaments or other political institutions,

—the power to engage in legal proceedings where the national provisions adopted pursuant to this Directive have been violated or to bring these violations to the attention of the judicial authorities.

Decisions by the supervisory authority which give rise to complaints may be appealed against through the courts.

4. Each supervisory authority shall hear claims lodged by any person, or by an association representing that person, concerning the protection of his rights and freedoms in regard to the processing of personal data. The person concerned shall be informed of the outcome of the claim.

Each supervisory authority shall, in particular, hear claims for checks on the lawfulness of data processing lodged by any person when the national provisions adopted pursuant to Article 13 of this Directive apply. The person shall at any rate be informed that a check has taken place.

5. Each supervisory authority shall draw up a report on its activities at regular intervals. The report shall be made public.

6. Each supervisory authority is competent, whatever the national law applicable to the processing in question, to exercise, on the territory of its own Member State, the powers conferred on it in accordance with paragraph 3. Each authority may be requested to exercise its powers by an authority of another Member State.

The supervisory authorities shall cooperate with one another to the extent necessary for the performance of their duties, in particular by exchanging all useful information.

7. Member States shall provide that the members and staff of the supervisory authority, even after their employment has ended, are to be subject to a

duty of professional secrecy with regard to confidential information to which they have access.

Article 29
Working Party on the Protection of Individuals with regard to the Processing of Personal Data

1. A Working Party on the Protection of Individuals with regard to the Processing of Personal Data, hereinafter referred to as "the Working Party," is hereby set up.
    It shall have advisory status and act independently.
2. The Working Party shall be composed of a representative of the supervisory authority or authorities designated by each Member State and of a representative of the authority or authorities established for the Community institutions and bodies, and of a representative of the Commission.
    Each member of the Working Party shall be designated by the institution, authority or authorities which he represents. Where a Member State has designated more than one supervisory authority, they shall nominate a joint representative. The same shall apply to the authorities established for Community institutions and bodies.
3. The Working Party shall take decisions by a simple majority of the representatives of the supervisory authorities.
4. The Working Party shall elect its chairman. The chairman's term of office shall be two years. His appointment shall be renewable.
5. The Working Party's secretariat shall be provided by the Commission.
6. The Working Party shall adopt its own rules of procedure.
7. The Working Party shall consider items placed on its agenda by its chairman, either on his own initiative or at the request of a representative of the supervisory authorities or at the Commission's request.

Article 30

1. The Working Party shall:
    (a) examine any question covering the application of the national measures adopted under this Directive in order to contribute to the uniform application of such measures;
    (b) give the Commission an opinion on the level of protection in the Community and in third countries;
    (c) advise the Commission on any proposed amendment of this Directive, on any additional or specific measures to safeguard the rights and freedoms of natural persons with regard to the processing of per-

sonal data and on any other proposed Community measures affecting such rights and freedoms;

(d) give an opinion on codes of conduct drawn up at Community level.

2. If the Working Party finds that divergences likely to affect the equivalence of protection for persons with regard to the processing of personal data in the Community are arising between the laws or practices of Member States, it shall inform the Commission accordingly.

3. The Working Party may, on its own initiative, make recommendations on all matters relating to the protection of persons with regard to the processing of personal data in the Community.

4. The Working Party's opinions and recommendations shall be forwarded to the Commission and to the committee referred to in Article 31.

5. The Commission shall inform the Working Party of the action it has taken in response to its opinions and recommendations. It shall do so in a report which shall also be forwarded to the European Parliament and the Council. The report shall be made public.

6. The Working Party shall draw up an annual report on the situation regarding the protection of natural persons with regard to the processing of personal data in the Community and in third countries, which it shall transmit to the Commission, the European Parliament and the Council. The report shall be made public.

Chapter VII: Community Implementing Measures

Article 31
The Committee

1. The Commission shall be assisted by a committee composed of the representatives of the Member States and chaired by the representative of the Commission.

2. The representative of the Commission shall submit to the committee a draft of the measures to be taken. The committee shall deliver its opinion on the draft within a time limit which the chairman may lay down according to the urgency of the matter.

The opinion shall be delivered by the majority laid down in Article 148 (2) of the Treaty. The votes of the representatives of the Member States within the committee shall be weighted in the manner set out in that Article. The chairman shall not vote.

The Commission shall adopt measures which shall apply immediately. However, if these measures are not in accordance with the opinion of the committee, they shall be communicated by the Commission to the Council forthwith. In that event:

—the Commission shall defer application of the measures which it has decided for a period of three months from the date of communication,

—the Council, acting by a qualified majority, may take a different decision within the time limit referred to in the first indent.

FINAL PROVISIONS

Article 32

1. Member States shall bring into force the laws, regulations and administrative provisions necessary to comply with this Directive at the latest at the end of a period of three years from the date of its adoption.

   When Member States adopt these measures, they shall contain a reference to this Directive or be accompanied by such reference on the occasion of their official publication. The methods of making such reference shall be laid down by the Member States.

2. Member States shall ensure that processing already under way on the date the national provisions adopted pursuant to this Directive enter into force, is brought into conformity with these provisions within three years of this date.

   By way of derogation from the preceding subparagraph, Member States may provide that the processing of data already held in manual filing systems on the date of entry into force of the national provisions adopted in implementation of this Directive shall be brought into conformity with Articles 6, 7 and 8 of this Directive within 12 years of the date on which it is adopted. Member States shall, however, grant the data subject the right to obtain, at his request and in particular at the time of exercising his right of access, the rectification, erasure or blocking of data which are incomplete, inaccurate or stored in a way incompatible with the legitimate purposes pursued by the controller.

3. By way of derogation from paragraph 2, Member States may provide, subject to suitable safeguards, that data kept for the sole purpose of historical research need not be brought into conformity with Articles 6, 7 and 8 of this Directive.

4. Member States shall communicate to the Commission the text of the provisions of domestic law which they adopt in the field covered by this Directive.

Article 33
The Commission shall report to the Council and the European Parliament at regular intervals, starting not later than three years after the date referred to in Article 32 (1), on the implementation of this Directive, attaching to its report, if necessary, suitable proposals for amendments. The report shall be made public.

The Commission shall examine, in particular, the application of this Directive to the data processing of sound and image data relating to natural persons and shall submit any appropriate proposals which prove to be necessary, taking account of developments in information technology and in the light of the state of progress in the information society.

Article 34
This Directive is addressed to the Member States.

Done at Luxembourg, 24 October 1995.
For the European Parliament
The President
K. HAENSCH
For the Council
The President
L. ATIENZA SERNA

∞

Bibliography

Note: References to legislation and case law were not included in this bibliography.

Alexander, C., and S. Gutwirth. *Te gek voor recht? De geesteszieke tussen recht en psychiatrie*, Tegenspraak Cahier nr. 17. Gent: Mys and Breesch, 1997.

Alston, P., and H. S. Steiner. *International Human Rights in Context: Law, Politics, Morals*. Oxford: Clarendon, 1996.

An-Na'Im, A. A. *Human Rights in Cross-cultural Perspective: A Quest for Consensus*. Philadelphia: University of Pennsylvania Press, 1992.

Aries, P., and G. Duby, eds. *Histoire de la vie privée*. 5 vols. Paris: Seuil. Vol. 1: *De l'empire romain à l'an mil*, sous la direction de P. Veyne, October 1985, 636; Vol. 2: *De l'Europe féodale à la Renaissance*, sous la direction de G. Duby, December 1985, 636; Vol. 3: *De la Renaissance aux Lumières*, sous la direction de R. Chartier, November 1986, 636; Vol. 4: *De la Révolution à la Grande Guerre*, sous la direction M. Perrot, November 1987, 637; and Vol. 5: *De la Première Guerre mondiale à nos jours*, sous la direction de A. Prost and G. Vincent, November 1987, 635.

Badinter, R. "Le droit au respect de la vie privée," *La semaine juridique*. I-Doctrine, 1968, nr. 2136.

Bell, D. *The Coming of Post-industrial Society: A Venture in Social Forecasting*. New York: Basic Books, 1976.

Boling, P. *Privacy and the Politics of Intimate Life*. Ithaca, N.Y.: Cornell University Press, 1996.

Boulanger, M.-H., C. De Terwangne, T. Leonard, S. Louveaux, D. Moreau, and Y. Poullet. "La protection des données à caractère personnel en droit communautaire," *Journal des tribunaux—Droit européen* (1997): 121–27.

Breton, P. *La tribu informatique. Enquête sur une passion moderne*. Paris: Métaillé, 1990.

Carbonnier, J. *Flexible droit. Textes pour une sociologie du droit sans rigueur.* 8th ed. Paris: L.G.D.J., 1995.

Cohen, S. "The Punitive City: Notes on the Dispersal of Social Control," *Contemporary Crises* (1979): 339–63.

————. *Visions of Social Control: Crime Punishment and Classification.* Cambridge: Polity/ Basil Blackwell, 1985.

Dandeker, C. *Surveillance, Power and Modernity.* Cambridge: Polity Press, 1990.

De Hert, P. "Oude en nieuwe wetgeving op controletechnieken in bedrijven," *Sociale kronieken,* no. 3 (1995): 105–18.

————. "Schending van het (tele)communicatiegeheim in het beroepsleven," *Tijdschrift voor sociaal recht,* no. 2 (1995): 213–93.

————. "Europese rechtspraak inzake dwangmiddelen, politietap, gevangenissen, politiegeweld, terrorisme, voorlopige hechtenis, anonieme getuigen, etc.," *Vigiles—Tijdschrift voor politierecht,* no. 3 (1996): 26–37.

————. "Camera's in bedrijven," *Oriëntatie,* no. 11 (1996): 200–208.

————. "European Data-Protection as a Potential Framework for Electronic Visual Surveillance." In *Proceedings of the First World Conference on New Trends in Criminal Investigation and Evidence,* edited by J. F. Nijboer and J. M. Reijntjes. Lelystad: Koninklijke Vermande, 1997, 557–68.

De Hert, P., O. De Schutter, and S. Gutwirth. "Pour une réglementation de la vidéosurveillance," *Journal des tribunaux* (1996): 569–79.

De Hert, P., and S. Gutwirth. "Controletechnieken op de werkplaats (deel 1): Een stand van zaken" en "Controletechnieken op de werkplaats (deel 2): Een herbeschouwing in het licht van het "persoonsgegevensbeschermingsrecht," *Oriëntatie,* no. 4 (1993): 93–109 and *Oriëntatie,* no. 5 (1993): 125–47.

————. "Cameratoezicht, veiligheid en de Wet Persoonsregistraties. Juridische denkoefeningen naar aanleiding van de Franse wet van 21 januari 1995 inzake veiligheid," *Recht en kritiek,* no. 3 (1995): 218–50.

Deleuze, G. *Pourparlers. 1972–1990.* Paris: Minuit, 1990.

Delmas-Marty, M. *Pour un droit commun.* Paris: Le Seuil/La librairie du XXe siècle, 1994.

De Schutter, B. "A Human Scientist Approach to Information Technology." In *Yearbook of Law, Computers and Technology,* vol. 3. London: Butterworths, 1987, 138–47.

————. "Europe's Data Protection Challenge," *Transnational Data and Communications Report* (January 1990): 15–16.

Dizard, W. P. *The Coming Information Age: An Overview of Technology, Economics, and Politics.* New York: Longman, 1989.

Donzelot, J. *La police des familles. Postface de Gilles Deleuze.* Paris: Minuit, 1977.

Doom, R., ed. *Tolerantie getolereerd? Islamitische en Westerse Opvattingen,* Tegenspraak Cahier 16. Gent: Mys and Breesch.

Elias, N. *Het civilisatieproces. Sociogenetische en psychogenetische onderzoekingen,* Utrecht: Spectrum-Aula paperback 148, 1987.

Ellul, J. *Le bluff technologique.* Paris: Hachette, 1987.

Ewald, F. *L'Etat providence*. Paris: Grasset, 1986.

Fauvet, J. "Le projet de Directive du Conseil des Ministres de la Communauté Européenne sur la protection des données personnelles." Paris: C.N.I.L., 1992.

Foqué, R. *De ruimte van het recht*. Arnhem: Gouda Quint, 1992.

Foqué, R., and A. C. 't Hart. *Instrumentaliteit en rechtsbescherming. Grondslagen van een strafrechtelijke waardendiscussie*. Arnhem/Antwerpen: Gouda Quint/Kluwer, 1990.

Foqué, R., and M. Weyemberg. *Filosofische aspecten van het privé-publiek debat*. Brussels: VUBPress, 1997.

Forester, T., ed. *The Information Technology Revolution*. Oxford: Blackwell, 1985.

Foucault, M. *Histoire de la folie à l'âge classique*. Paris: Gallimard, 1972.

———. *Surveiller et punir. Naissance de la prison*. Paris: Gallimard, 1975.

———. *Histoire de la sexualité 1. La volonté de savoir*. Paris: Gallimard, 1976.

———. *Histoire de la sexualité 2. L'usage des plaisirs*. Paris: Gallimard, 1984.

———. *Histoire de la sexualité 3. Le souci de soi*. Paris: Gallimard, 1984.

———. "Deux essais sur le sujet et le pouvoir." In *Michel Foucault: Un parcours philosophique*, edited by H. Dreyfus and P. Rabinow. Paris: Gallimard, 1984, 297–321.

Franck, T. M. "Postmodern Tribalism and the Right to Secession" and "Comments by R. Higgins." In *Peoples and Minorities in International Law*, edited by C. M. Brolman, R. Lefeber, and M. Y. A. Zieck. Dordrecht: Martinus Nijhoff, 1993, 3–27, 29–35.

———. *Fairness in International Law and Institutions*. Oxford: Clarendon Press, 1995.

Galenkamp, M. *Individualism versus Collectivism: The Concept of Collective Rights*. Rotterdam: RFS, 1993.

Ganshof Van der Meersch, W. G. "Propos sur le texte de la loi et les principes généraux du droit," *Journal des tribunaux* (1970): 557–74, 581–96.

———. "Le respect des droits fondamentaux de l'homme, condition exigée du droit des états européens," *Revue de droit international et comparé* (1983): 9–30.

Giddens, A. *A Contemporary Critique of Historical Materialism*, vol. 1: *Power, Property and the State*. London: Macmillan, 1983.

Guldix, E. *De persoonlijkheidsrechten, de persoonlijke levenssfeer en het privéleven in hun onderling verband*. Doctoraatsproefschrift—VUB, 1986.

Gutwirth, S. *Waarheidsaanspraken in recht en wetenschap. Een onderzoek naar de verhouding tussen recht en wetenschap met bijzondere illustraties uit het informaticarecht*. Brussel/Antwerpen: VUBPress/MAKLU, 1993.

———. "De toepassing van het finaliteitsbeginsel van de Privacywet van 8 december 1992 tot bescherming van de persoonlijke levenssfeer ten opzichte van de verwerking van persoonsgegevens," *Tijdschrift voor privaatrecht*, no. 4 (1993): 1409–77.

———. "De ontdekking van de privacy van de burgers als doeltreffend wapen in de strijd tussen concurrenten," *Handelspraktijken en mededinging—Jaarboek 1994*, edited by H. De Bauw. Kluwer rechtswetenschappen, 1995, 372–91. Noot bij Voorz. Kh. Brussel, 15 September 1994.

———. "Nineteen Ninety-Five! Hoog tijd om cameratoezicht te beperken" (Redactioneel), *Recht en kritiek*, no. 1 (1995) 3–11.

———. "Het harlekijnspak en het vale ezelsvel. Individuele vrijheden in de greep van het recht op zelfbeschikking van volken, het nationalisme en andere aanspraken op een collectieve identiteit." In *Naar een nieuwe interpretatie van het recht op zelfbeschikking?* edited by N. Sybesma and J. Van Bellingen. Brussels, Belgium: VUBPress, 1995, 53–88.

Haarscher, G. *Philosophie des droits de l'homme.* Brussels: Editions de l'ULB, 1987.

Hamelink, C. *Informatie en macht.* Baarn: Anthos, 1984.

———. *The Technology Gamble.* Norwood: ABLEX, 1988.

't Hart, A. C. *Recht als schild van Perseus. Voordrachten over strafrechtstheorie.* Leerstoel Theodore Verhaegen 1989–1990-Vrije Universiteit Brussel. Arnhem/Antwerpen: Gouda Quint/Kluwer, 1991.

———. *Mensenwerk? Over rechtsbegrip en mensbeeld in het strafrecht van de democratische rechtsstaat,* Mededelingen van de Koninklijke Nederlandse Akademie van Wetenschappen, Afdeling Letterkunde, Noord-Hollandsche. Amsterdam: Nieuwe reeks, 1995 Deel 58, no. 4.

———. *De meerwaarde van het strafrecht.* Den Haag: SDU, 1997.

Het recht op privacy en de sluiers van het recht. Tegenspraak Cahiers 5. Antwerpen: Kluwer, 1988.

Hulsman, B. J. *Als de telefoon wordt opgenomen. Regels voor het registreren, meeluisteren en opnemen van telefoongesprekken van werknemers.* Den Haag, Netherlands: Registratiekamer, November 1996.

Ippel, P., G. De Heij, and B. Crouwers, eds. *Privacy Disputed.* Den Haag: SDU, 1995.

Jacobs, K. "Genetische informatie en verzekeringen," *Recht en kritiek,* no. 1 (1997): 16–38.

Krings, E. "Allocution de cloture," *Annales de droit de Louvain,* no. 1–2 (1984): 427–34.

Latour, B. *Wetenschap in actie.* Amsterdam: Bert Bakker, 1988.

———. *Nous n'avons jamais été modernes. Essai d'anthropologie symétrique.* Paris: La Découverte, 1991.

Levy, P. *La machine univers. Création, cognition et culture informatique.* Paris: La Découverte, 1987.

———. *Les technologies de l'intelligence. L'avenir de la pensée à l'ère informatique.* Paris: La Découverte, 1990.

Loschak, D. "Mutation des droits de l'homme et mutation du droit," *Revue interdisciplinaire d'études juridiques,* nr. 13 (1984): 49–89.

Luney, P. R., and K. Takahashi, eds. *Japanese Constitutional Law.* Tokyo: University of Tokyo Press, 1993.

Lyon, D. "Benthams Panopticon: From Moral Architecture to Electronic Surveillance," *Queens Quarterly,* vol. 98 (1991): 596–617.

———. *The Electronic Eye: The Rise of Surveillance Society.* Cambridge: Polity Press, 1994.

Lyon, D., and E. Zureik, eds. *Computers, Surveillance, and Privacy.* Madison: University of Minnesota Press, 1996.

Marx, G. T. "La société de sécurité maximale," *Déviance et société* (1988): 147–66.

———. "Privacy and Technology," *The World and I* (September 1990): 523–41.

―――. "Electric Eye in the Sky: Some Reflections on the New Surveillance and Popular Culture." In *Computers, Surveillance, and Privacy*, edited by D. Lyon and E. Zureik. Madison: University of Minnesota Press, 1996.

Marx, G. T., and N. Reichman. "Routinizing the Discovery of Secrets: Computers as Informants," *American Behavioral Scientist*, vol. 27 (1984): 423–52.

Masuda, Y. "Vision of the Global Information Society." In *Information Technology: Impact on the Way of Life*, edited by L. Bannon. Conference on the Information Society. Dublin: Tycooly, 1982.

―――. "Computopia." In *The Information Technology Revolution*, edited by T. Forester. Oxford: Blackwell, 1985.

Mayer, A. E. *Islam and Human Rights*. Boulder, Colo.: Westview Press, 1995.

Mbaye, K. *Les droits de l'homme en Afrique*. Paris: Pedone, 1992.

McLean, D. *Privacy and Its Invasion*. London: Praeger, 1995.

Mortier, F. "Waarom privacy belangrijk is. Een sociogenetisch standpunt." In *Het recht op privacy en de sluiers van het recht*, Tegenspraak Cahiers 5. Antwerpen: Kluwer, 1988.

Nabben, P. F. P., and H. J. M. L.Van de Luytgaarden. *De ultieme vrijheid. Een rechtstheoretische analyse van het recht op privacy*. Deventer: Kluwer, 1996.

Nora, S., and A. Minc. *L'informatisation de la société*. Paris: La Documentation Française/ Seuil, Points Politique 92.

Oda, H. *Japanese Law*. London: Butterworths, 1992.

Ouguergouz, F. *La Charte africaine des droits de l'homme et des peuples. Une approche juridique des droits de l'homme entre tradition et modernité*. Paris: PUF, 1993.

Overkleeft-Verburg, G. *De wet persoonsregistraties. Norm, toepassing en evaluatie*. Zwolle: Tjeenk Willink, 1995.

Petrella, R., en de Groep van Lissabon, *Grenzen aan de concurrentie*, Maatschappij en technisch-wetenschappelijke ontwikkelingen–1. Brussels: VUBPress, 1994.

Petrella, R. *Het algemeen belang. Lof van de solidariteit*, Maatschappij en technisch-wetenschappelijke ontwikkelingen–4. Brussels: VUBPress, 1997.

Pettiti, L.-E., E. Decaux, and P.-H. Imbert. *La Convention européenne des droits de l'homme. Commentaire article par article*. Paris: Economica, 1995.

Poullet, Y. "Data Protection between Property and Liberties: A Civil Approach." In *Amongst Friends in Computers and Law: A Collection of Essays in Remembrance of Guy Vandenberghe*, edited by H. W. K. Kaspersen and A. Oskamp. Computer/Law series, nr. 8. Deventer: Kluwer, 1990, 162–81.

Poullet, Y. "Le fondement du droit à la protection des données nominatives: 'propriétés ou libertés.'" In *Nouvelles technologies et propriétés*, edited by E. MacKaay (1989), 175–203.

Poullet, Y., and T. Leonard. "Les libertés comme fondement de la protection des données nominatives." In *La vie privée. Une liberté parmi les autres?* edited by F. Rigaux. Namur/ Brussels: Travaux de la faculté de droit de Namur/ Larcier, 1992.

Raes, K. "Homo Incognitus. Het recht op privacy en de ethiek van de gespleten mens." In *Het recht op privacy en de sluiers van het recht*, Tegenspraak Cahiers 5. Antwerpen: Kluwer, 1988.

————. "The Privacy of Technology and the Technology of Privacy: The Rise of Privatism and the Deprivation of Public Culture." In *High Technology and Law: A Critical Approach*, edited by A. Sajo and F. Petrik, 73–100. Budapest: Institute of Political and Legal Sciences, Academy of Sciences, 1989.

————. "De universele strekking en de contextuele variabiliteit van mensenrechten." In *Van wereldburger tot "bange blanke man,"* edited by H. Corijn, 91–115. Brussels, Belgium: VUBPress, 1994.

Registratiekamer. *In beeld gebracht. Privacyregels voor het gebruik van videocamera's voor toezicht en beveiliging.* Registratiekamer (januari 1997).

————. *Wet bescherming persoonsgegevens. Advies van de Registratiekamer* (februari 1997).

Rigaux, F. "La conception occidentale des droits fondamentaux face à l'Islam," *Revue trimestrielle des droits de l'homme* (1990): 105–23.

————. *La protection de la vie privée et des autres biens de la personnalité.* Brussels: Bruylant/L.G.D.J, 1990.

————. "La liberté de la vie privée," *Revue internationale de droit comparé* (1991): 539–63.

————. *La vie privée. Une liberté parmi les autres?*, avec les contributions de Y. Poullet, X. Thunis, and T. Leonard. Brussels: Chaire Francqui/Travaux de la faculté de droit de Namur, Larcier, 1992.

————. "Justice et presse: réflexions comparatives," *Journal des tribunaux* (1996): 41–46.

Roszak, T. *The Cult of Information: The Folklore of Computers and the True Art of Thinking.* London: Paladin, 1986.

Rouland, N. *Aux confins du droit. Anthropologie juridique de la modernité.* Paris: Odile Jacob, 1991.

Rozemond, K. "Charles Z. en de gerechtelijke normering van buitenwettelijke opsporingsmethoden." *Recht en kritiek*, no. 1 (1997): 39–70.

Rubenfeld, J. "The Right of Privacy," *Harvard Law Review*, vol. 102 (1989): 737–807.

Sajo, A., and F. Petrik, eds. *High Technology and Law: A Critical Approach.* Budapest: Institute of Political and Legal Sciences—Academy of Sciences, 1989.

Schiller, H. *Who Knows? Information in the Age of the Fortune 500.* Norwood, N.J.: ABLEX, 1982.

Serres, M. *Hermès V: Le passage du Nord-Ouest.* Paris: Minuit, 1980.

————. *Le Tiers-Instruit.* Paris: François Bourin, 1991.

————. "Préface: appartenance et identité." In *Les arbres de connaissance*, edited by M. Authier and P. Levy, 7–15. Paris: La Découverte, 1992.

————. *Eclaircissements. Entretiens avec Bruno Latour.* Paris: François Bourin, 1992.

————, ed. *Eléments d'histoire des sciences.* Paris: Bordas, 1989.

Spier, J. T. Hartlief, G. E. Van Maanen, and R. D. Vriesendorp. *Verbintenissen uit de wet en schadevergoeding.* Deventer: Kluwer, 1997.

Stengers, I. *L'invention des sciences modernes.* Paris: La Découverte, 1993.

————. *Macht en wetenschappen*, Maatschappij en technisch-wetenschappelijke ontwikkelingen – 5. Brussels: VUBPress, 1997.

Touraine, A. *Qu'est-ce la démocratie?* Paris: Fayard, 1994.

———. *Pourrons-nous vivre ensemble? Egaux et différents*. Paris: Fayard, 1997.

Tribe, L. H. *American Constitutional Law*. New York: Foundation Press, 1988.

Tribe, L. H., and M. C. Dorf. *On Reading the Constitution*. Cambridge, Mass.: Harvard University Press, 1991.

Van Gerven, W. *Hoe blauw is het bloed van de prins?* Netherlands: Kluwer, Rechtswetenschappen, 1983.

———. "Principe de proportionnalité, abus de droit et droits fondamentaux," *Journal des tribunaux* (1992): 305–9.

Verhey, L. F. M. *Horizontale werking van grondrechten, in het bijzonder van het recht op privacy*. Zwolle, Netherlands: Tjeenk Willink, 1992.

Vitalis, A. *Informatique, pouvoir et libertés*. Paris: Economica, 1988.

———. "De EG-richtlijn bescherming persoonsgegevens: uitgangspunten en hoofdlijnen," *NCJM-Bulletin*, vol. 22, no. 3 (1997): 239–56.

Voorhoof, D. "De vrijheid van expressie en informatie en de rechtspraak van de ECRM en het EHRM betreffende artikel 10 EVRM (1958–1994)," *Mediaforum*, no. 11–12 (1994): 116–24.

Wacks, R. *Personal Information: Privacy and the Law*. Oxford: Clarendon Press, 1989.

Warren, S. D., and L. D. Brandeis. "The Right to Privacy," *Harvard Law Review*, vol. 4 (1890): 193–220.

Webster, F., and K. Robins. *Information Technology: A Luddite Analysis*. Norwood, N.J.: ABLEX, 1986.

Weizenbaum, J. *Computerkracht en mensenmacht. Van oordeel tot berekening*. Amsterdam: Contact, 1984.

Willekens, H. "Het grondrecht op privacy, de afbakening van de privé-sfeer en publieke sfeer en de maatschappelijke allocatie van bestaansmiddelen." In *Het recht op privacy en de sluier van het recht*, Tegenspraak Cahiers 5, 47–71. Antwerp, Belgium: Kluwer, 1988.

———. *Recht op privacy en kapitalistische markteconomie. Kritische bedenkingen bij de privacyregulering, in het bijzonder bij de wet van 8 december 1992 tot bescherming van de persoonlijke levenssfeer, dactyl.* 1997, forthcoming.

Winner, L. *Autonomous Technology: Technics-out-of-Control as a Theme of Political Thought*. Cambridge: MIT Press, 1977.

Index

∞

About the Author and the Rathenau Institute

Serge Gutwirth teaches theory and philosophy of law, comparative law, and human rights at the Free University of Brussels (Belgium) and the Erasmus University Rotterdam (The Netherlands). Both as an independent researcher and as a promoter of research, Gutwirth works on subjects concerning the relationship between law and technological and scientific developments. He is mainly interested in the safeguarding of personal freedom and privacy in a society that is increasingly being influenced by the rise of information technologies. Gutwirth is the author of three monographs in Dutch: *Dostojevsky criminoloog?* (1985), *Waarheidsaanspraken in recht en wetenschap* (1993), and *Privacyvrijheid!* (1998). As an editor or coeditor he is responsible for, among others, *Quel avenir pour le droit de l'environnement?* (1996), *Te gek voor recht? De gesteszieke tussen recht en psychiatrie* (1997), *Science, Technology and Social Change: The Orange Book of Einstein Meets Magritte* (1999), and *Vraagstukken van milieurechthelijke begripsvorming* (2000). Gutwirth has contributed to a great variety of international scientific journals.

Technological and scientific developments often give rise to political and societal concerns. The **Rathenau Institute,** the Dutch national technology assessment organization, assists both government and the general public in forming a soundly based judgment on these matters by prompting discussions between various parties concerned and by setting up research activities.

151

Through its activities, the institute constitutes a cohesive element among politics, science, and society. The results of the institute's projects are presented to the Dutch Parliament. The Rathenau Institute is an independent organization that advises the Dutch Parliament and is one of the institutes of the Royal Netherlands Academy of Arts and Sciences.